RYAN WILDER
TRAVEL GUIDE

to

ISTANBUL,
TURKEY

By Ryan Wilder

Copywright & Disclaimer

Copyright © 2025

Disclaimer

The information provided in this book is for general guidance and informational purposes only. While every effort has been made to ensure accuracy and thoroughness, the author and publisher make no representations or warranties of any kind, express or implied, about the completeness, accuracy, reliability, suitability, or availability of the content.

The author shall not be held responsible for any errors, omissions, or inaccuracies, nor for any loss, injury, inconvenience, or damage resulting from the use or reliance upon the information contained in this guide. Travelers are encouraged to verify any details, such as travel restrictions, costs, and local regulations, before embarking on their journey.

By using this guide, you agree that the author will not be held liable for any direct or indirect damages arising from its use.

Table of Contents

Introduction To Istanbul

Welcome To Istanbul

Istanbul, Turkey's largest city, is a place where two continents meet, Europe and Asia. It is one of the most fascinating cities in the world, rich with history, culture, and stunning landmarks. Istanbul is unique because it is the only city that spans two continents, separated by the Bosphorus Strait. This city offers a mix of old and new, blending ancient traditions with modern life. Whether you are walking along cobblestone streets, exploring grand mosques, or sipping coffee in a trendy café, Istanbul will captivate you with its charm.

Istanbul is often referred to as "the city that never sleeps." This is because it is always alive with activity, from early morning until late at night. The city welcomes millions of visitors every year, offering a wide range of experiences. From historical monuments to vibrant markets, from Turkish baths to delicious food, Istanbul provides something for everyone.

History And Culture

Istanbul has a long and rich history that dates back over 2,500 years. Originally known as Byzantium, it was founded by the Greeks in the 7th century BC. The city was later renamed Constantinople after Emperor Constantine, who made it the capital of the Roman Empire in 330 AD. Constantinople continued to be the capital of the Byzantine Empire until it fell to the Ottoman Turks in 1453. The Ottomans transformed the city, turning it into the heart of their vast empire for over 400 years.

Throughout its history, Istanbul has been a melting pot of cultures. It has been influenced by the ancient Greeks, Romans, Byzantines, and Ottomans, and each of these civilizations left their mark on the city's architecture, art, and culture. This blend of influences has given Istanbul its distinctive identity, combining European and Asian elements in a way that no other city can match.

Today, Istanbul is a modern metropolis, but its historical roots are still visible. The city is home to many iconic historical sites such as the Hagia Sophia, Topkapi Palace, and the Blue Mosque, which reflect its diverse heritage. The culture of Istanbul is also a mix of the traditional and the contemporary. The old world charm of the Grand Bazaar and spice markets contrasts with the stylish cafes and restaurants in neighborhoods like Beyoğlu and Karaköy.

Overview Of Istanbul

Istanbul is a city that effortlessly blends the old and the new, with a rich cultural heritage and a modern, vibrant atmosphere. The city is divided into two main parts: the European side and the Asian side. The European side is home to most of the city's historical landmarks, such as the Hagia Sophia, Topkapi Palace, and the Sultanahmet area, where the famous Blue Mosque stands. On this side of the city, you will also find lively neighborhoods like Beyoğlu, where you can explore modern art galleries, boutique shops, and bustling streets.

The Asian side of Istanbul offers a more relaxed and local atmosphere. Here, you'll find charming neighborhoods such as Kadıköy and Üsküdar, known for their parks, markets, and local cafés. The Asian side is less touristy and provides a more authentic experience of Istanbul life. Visitors to the Asian side can enjoy scenic views of the Bosphorus Strait and experience a slower pace of life compared to the busy European side.

Istanbul is also famous for its incredible food scene. Turkish cuisine is full of rich flavors and diverse dishes, from kebabs and baklava to mezze and Turkish delight. The city has an array of dining options, from street food stalls offering delicious simit (Turkish bagel) and döner kebabs to high-end restaurants serving gourmet Turkish and international cuisine.

Istanbul is also a city of contrasts. On one hand, it is modern and progressive, with a thriving arts and culture scene, luxury shopping malls, and trendy neighborhoods. On the other hand, it is steeped in tradition, with historical sites, ancient mosques, and charming bazaars. It is a city where East meets West, and where the past and present coexist in harmony.

How To Get To Istanbul

By Air

Istanbul is served by two major airports, making air travel to the city very convenient for international and domestic visitors. The two airports are:

Istanbul Airport (IST)

Istanbul Airport is the main international airport and one of the busiest airports in the world. It is located on the European side of Istanbul, around 40 kilometers (25 miles) from the city center. This airport is well-connected with direct flights from almost every major city worldwide, making it a key entry point for international travelers. It offers plenty of amenities such as duty-free shops, lounges, restaurants, and currency exchange services.

- **Address:** Istanbul Airport, Arnavutköy, 34283 Istanbul, Turkey
- **Phone Number:** +90 444 1 440

Sabiha Gökçen International Airport (SAW)

Sabiha Gökçen is the second international airport in Istanbul, located on the Asian side of the city, approximately 35 kilometers (22 miles) from the city center. This airport is typically used by low-cost carriers and has a growing number of international and domestic flights. While smaller than Istanbul Airport, Sabiha Gökçen still offers modern facilities and easy access to the city via public transportation or taxi.

- **Address:** Sabiha Gökçen International Airport, Pendik, 34912 Istanbul, Turkey
- **Phone Number:** +90 216 588 88 88

Once you arrive at either airport, you can use taxis, shuttle buses, or the metro (from Istanbul Airport) to reach the city center. Taxis from the airport to central areas like Sultanahmet or Taksim cost around 200-300 TRY depending on traffic and the destination.

By Sea

Istanbul, surrounded by the Bosphorus, the Sea of Marmara, and the Golden Horn, is a city where water transport plays a significant role in daily life. Many visitors and locals use ferries to travel between different parts of the city, and traveling by sea can be a scenic and enjoyable way to arrive.

Ferries to Istanbul

If you are coming from nearby countries or cities around the Sea of Marmara, such as Bursa or Yalova, you can travel to Istanbul by ferry. Ferries from Greece, specifically from islands like Thessaloniki and Chios, also arrive at Istanbul's ports.

- **Main Ferry Ports in Istanbul:**

- **Emin Ali Paşa Port** (close to Sultanahmet)
- **Karaköy Port**
- **Kadıköy Port** (Asian side)

Cruise Ships

Istanbul is a popular stop for Mediterranean and Aegean Sea cruises. Cruise ships often dock at the **Galataport** cruise terminal, located near Karaköy, close to many attractions like the Galata Tower and the Bosphorus. The cruise terminal is equipped with modern facilities, and passengers can easily access taxis or the tram to get around the city.

- **Address:** Galataport, Tophane, 34425 Istanbul, Turkey
- **Phone Number:** +90 212 343 55 00

Traveling by sea is a relaxing option and provides beautiful views of the city from the water.

By Land

Istanbul is well-connected by road and rail to other parts of Turkey and neighboring countries. Whether you are traveling by bus, car, or train, getting to Istanbul by land is an easy and convenient option.

By Bus

Istanbul has several long-distance bus terminals, with buses arriving from various parts of Turkey as well as countries such as Greece, Bulgaria, and Iran. The two main bus stations in Istanbul are:

Esenler Bus Terminal: The largest bus station in Istanbul, serving intercity buses. Located on the European side, it connects to various parts of Turkey and beyond.

- **Address:** Esenler Otogarı, 34410 Istanbul, Turkey
- **Phone Number:** +90 212 659 34 42

Harem Bus Terminal: Located on the Asian side of Istanbul, this terminal serves buses coming from the southern regions of Turkey and neighboring countries.

- **Address:** Harem Otogarı, 34716 Istanbul, Turkey
- **Phone Number:** +90 216 494 44 00

Buses are a popular choice for travelers looking for budget-friendly options. They are comfortable and affordable, with many services running overnight.

By Car

Driving into Istanbul is possible from neighboring countries, especially if you're coming from Europe via Bulgaria or Greece. There are well-maintained highways connecting Istanbul to other Turkish cities like Ankara and İzmir. While renting a car is an option, traffic in Istanbul can be heavy, and parking is limited in busy areas. If you plan to drive, it's best to stay on the highways and use public transport or taxis once you're within the city.

By Train

Istanbul is connected to other cities in Turkey and some neighboring countries via the rail network. The city's main train station is **Sirkeci Station** on the European side, which is connected to destinations like Edirne, Sofia, and Bucharest. However, Turkey's rail system is currently being modernized, so be sure to check train schedules and availability before planning your trip.

- **Address:** Sirkeci Railway Station, 34112 Istanbul, Turkey
- **Phone Number:** +90 212 520 08 83

Visa And Entry Requirements

When traveling to Istanbul, it is important to understand the visa and entry requirements. Citizens of many countries can enter Turkey with a visa, which can be obtained in different ways depending on your nationality.

Visa for Tourists

Most travelers from European, North American, and Asian countries need a visa to enter Turkey. Many travelers can apply for an **e-Visa** online before their trip. This is a simple process, and you'll need to provide basic information, such as your passport details, and pay a small fee. You can apply for an e-Visa through the official website:

Visa on Arrival

In some cases, travelers can obtain a visa on arrival at the airport. However, this option is available only for citizens of specific countries, so it's recommended to check if you are eligible before you travel.

Visa Exempt Countries

Some countries' citizens are exempt from needing a visa for stays of up to 90 days. This includes citizens from countries like Japan, South Korea, and many other European countries. Check the Turkish government website or the nearest Turkish embassy for more detailed information.

Passport Requirements

Your passport should be valid for at least 6 months beyond your arrival date in Turkey. Be sure to check the expiration date before applying for your visa or traveling.

Best Time to Visit and Duration of Stay

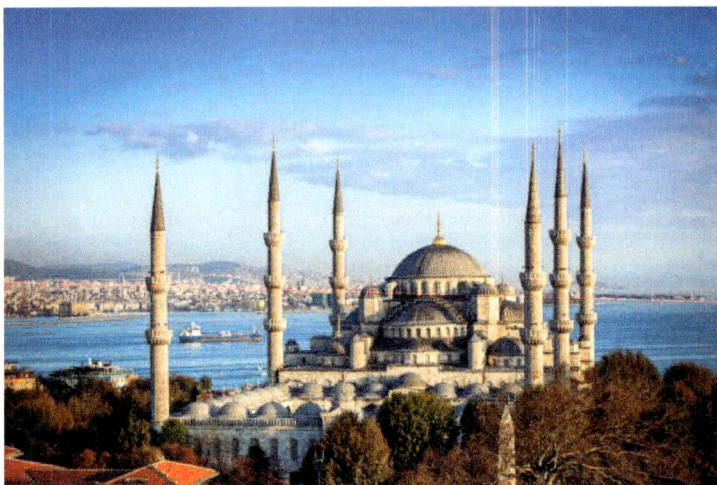

Climate Overview

Istanbul has a **temperate climate**, meaning it experiences distinct seasons throughout the year. The weather can change dramatically depending on the time of year, so understanding the climate will help you decide when to visit.

Spring (March to May)

Spring is one of the best times to visit Istanbul. During these months, the weather is mild, with daytime temperatures ranging from 10°C (50°F) to 20°C (68°F). It's neither too hot nor too cold, which makes it perfect for sightseeing and exploring the city's outdoor attractions, such as parks and the Bosphorus. You can also enjoy the vibrant colors of flowers blooming in the gardens and streets.

Summer (June to August)

Summer in Istanbul can get quite hot, especially in July and August. Temperatures often range from 25°C (77°F) to 30°C (86°F), but they can occasionally go higher. The heat can be intense, particularly in the afternoons, but this is also when the city sees the most tourists. If you enjoy warm weather and outdoor festivals, summer could be a great time to visit. However, be prepared for crowded attractions and higher hotel prices.

Autumn (September to November)

Autumn is another great time to visit Istanbul. The temperatures begin to cool down, ranging from 15°C (59°F) to 25°C (77°F), making it comfortable for outdoor activities and sightseeing. The fall colors around the parks and along the Bosphorus add to the beauty of the city. It's also a less crowded time compared to summer, so you can enjoy the city's attractions more peacefully.

Winter (December to February)

Winter in Istanbul is cold and rainy. The temperatures typically range from 5°C (41°F) to 10°C (50°F), but it can feel colder with the wind. Snow is possible, though it's not very common. The winter months see fewer tourists, making it a quieter time to visit. If you don't mind the chill, winter can be a peaceful time to explore the city's indoor attractions, such as museums and palaces. Plus, the lower number of tourists means you can enjoy a more relaxed experience.

Peak And Off-peak Seasons

Peak Season (June to August)

The peak season in Istanbul is during the summer months, especially June, July, and August. This is when most tourists from all over the world visit the city. The weather is warm and ideal for outdoor activities, and the city hosts various festivals and events.

However, the downside of visiting during this time is that attractions can be crowded, and prices for hotels and flights tend to be higher. If you don't mind the crowds and want to experience Istanbul at its most vibrant, summer could be the time for you.

Shoulder Season (March to May and September to November)

The best time to visit Istanbul is typically in the spring (March to May) and autumn (September to November). These are considered the shoulder seasons, where you'll find a good balance between pleasant weather, fewer tourists, and more affordable prices. During these times, you can enjoy the city's main attractions without dealing with long lines and large crowds. The weather is mild, making it perfect for exploring the city on foot. Many travelers find this to be the ideal time to visit because it offers the best of both worlds: enjoyable weather and a more relaxed atmosphere.

Off-Peak Season (December to February)

The off-peak season in Istanbul falls in the winter months, from December to February. While the weather is cold and there's a chance of rain or snow, the city is less crowded, which can make for a more peaceful experience. If you don't mind the cooler weather, winter can be a wonderful time to visit the city's museums, palaces, and indoor attractions. Prices for flights and hotels are generally lower during this time, which makes it more affordable for those on a budget. However, be aware that some outdoor activities, like Bosphorus cruises, may not operate during this period due to the cold or weather conditions.

Recommended Duration Of Stay

Short Stay (3-4 Days)

If you're only visiting Istanbul for a few days, you can still see the main attractions in a short amount of time. In 3 to 4 days, you can explore iconic landmarks such as:

- **Hagia Sophia:** A historic site that has served as a church, mosque, and museum.
- **Topkapi Palace:** The grand palace of Ottoman sultans.
- **Blue Mosque:** A stunning mosque with beautiful blue tiles.
- **Basilica Cistern:** An ancient underground water storage system.
- **Grand Bazaar and Spice Bazaar:** Great places for shopping and experiencing the local culture.

A 3-4 day visit allows you to see the highlights of the city but will be more rushed if you try to explore in-depth or venture outside the main tourist areas.

Medium Stay (5-7 Days)

For a more comfortable experience where you can explore more of the city's neighborhoods, historical sites, and local spots, a stay of 5 to 7 days is ideal. This gives you time to enjoy the city at a slower pace, visit museums, explore local markets, and maybe even take a ferry across the Bosphorus to visit the Asian side of Istanbul. You'll also have time to visit less touristy areas like the neighborhoods of Kadıköy and Üsküdar on the Asian side or the vibrant districts of Karaköy and Beyoğlu on the European side.

Long Stay (8-10 Days or More)

If you have more time, such as a week or more, you can fully immerse yourself in Istanbul's culture and history. You can take day trips to nearby areas like **Bursa** or **Edirne**, or even enjoy a boat tour along the Bosphorus. You'll have time to visit more museums, explore Istanbul's rich food scene, relax in local cafés, and discover hidden gems in the city. For those who want to experience both the historical side of Istanbul and the modern, vibrant lifestyle, 8 to 10 days is the perfect amount of time to get a deep sense of the city.

Practical Information

Currency And Banking

Istanbul uses the **Turkish Lira (TRY)** as its official currency. While some places may accept foreign currencies like the Euro or US Dollar, it's generally best to use the local currency for most transactions, especially in local markets, small shops, and restaurants.

Currency Exchange

You can exchange your money for Turkish Lira at various places in Istanbul, such as:

- **Currency exchange offices (Döviz Bürosu):** These can be found throughout the city, especially in tourist areas like Sultanahmet, Taksim, and near major transportation hubs like airports and train stations.
- **Banks:** Many banks in Istanbul offer currency exchange services, though the rates may be slightly less favorable compared to dedicated exchange offices. Major banks like **Garanti Bank**, **Yapı Kredi**, and **Ziraat Bank** are commonly found throughout the city.
- **ATMs:** There are plenty of ATMs around Istanbul where you can withdraw Turkish Lira using your debit or credit card. Most ATMs charge a fee for foreign cards, so check with your bank about any additional charges.

Credit and Debit Cards

Credit and debit cards (Visa and MasterCard are the most widely accepted) are accepted in many places, especially in tourist areas, hotels, larger shops, and restaurants. However, it's a good idea to carry some cash for small purchases, local markets, or for when you visit smaller shops and cafés that may not accept cards.

Tipping

Tipping is common in Istanbul but not obligatory. In restaurants, a tip of around 5-10% of the total bill is appreciated, especially if the service has been good. It's also common to leave a small tip for hotel staff, taxi drivers, and tour guides. However, always check if a service charge is included in the bill before tipping.

Time Zone

Istanbul is located in the **Turkey Time Zone (TRT)**, which is **GMT+3**. This means it is 3 hours ahead of Greenwich Mean Time (GMT).

Turkey does not observe **Daylight Saving Time (DST)**, so the time remains the same throughout the year. Whether you're visiting in summer or winter, there will be no time changes to worry about.

It's important to keep the time zone in mind when planning any communication with people back home or making appointments for tours, transportation, or other services. Many international travelers find it helpful to set their phone or devices to Istanbul's local time as soon as they arrive to avoid confusion.

Health And Safety Tips

Istanbul is generally a safe city for tourists, but like any major city, it's important to take some health and safety precautions to ensure a pleasant experience. Here are some tips to help you stay safe and healthy:

Health Tips

- **Tap Water:** The tap water in Istanbul is treated and generally safe to drink, but many locals and tourists prefer to drink bottled water for taste and convenience. Bottled water is widely available and affordable in shops and restaurants.
- **Food Safety:** Istanbul offers an abundance of street food, which is delicious but can sometimes cause stomach discomfort if you're not used to the local food. Stick to freshly prepared food from busy stalls, and avoid anything that looks like it has been sitting out for a long time.
- **Vaccinations:** Before traveling to Istanbul, it's a good idea to check with your healthcare provider about recommended vaccinations, particularly if you're traveling from a country where certain diseases are prevalent. Common travel vaccinations include Hepatitis A, Hepatitis B, and Typhoid.
- **Pharmacies:** Pharmacies are widely available throughout the city, and they often provide over-the-counter medication for minor illnesses such as colds, headaches, and stomach problems. If you need a prescription or more specialized treatment, you can visit a doctor or a hospital.

Safety Tips

- **Scams:** While Istanbul is relatively safe, it's always good to be cautious of potential scams, especially in crowded areas or popular tourist spots. Be wary of people offering unsolicited help, overly eager vendors, or anyone asking you to join them for private tours.

- **Pickpockets:** Like in any major city, pickpocketing can happen, especially in crowded places like public transportation, markets, or popular tourist attractions. Keep your valuables close, such as in a zipped bag or front pocket, and avoid carrying too much cash.
- **Solo Travelers:** Istanbul is generally safe for solo travelers, but it's still wise to stick to well-lit areas and avoid wandering through unfamiliar or less populated streets late at night.

Public Transportation Safety:

Istanbul's public transportation system, including buses, ferries, trams, and the metro, is very safe, but it can be crowded, especially during rush hours. Always keep an eye on your belongings, and be prepared for busy travel times. For added convenience, consider using an **Istanbulkart** (a travel card) to easily pay for rides on public transport.

Emergency Services

In case of an emergency, Istanbul has reliable services for health, safety, and general assistance. Here are the important emergency contacts you should know while visiting:

Police:

If you need to contact the police for any reason, dial **155**. The police in Istanbul are generally friendly and helpful, and English-speaking officers can sometimes be found in tourist areas.

Ambulance and Medical Assistance:

For any medical emergency, you can reach an ambulance by dialing **112**. This number will connect you to emergency medical services, including ambulances, fire services, and rescue teams.

Fire Department:

In case of a fire, dial **110** to contact the fire department.

Hospitals and Medical Centers:

Istanbul has many hospitals and medical centers offering high-quality healthcare services. Some well-known hospitals include:

- **American Hospital (Amerikan Hastanesi)**
  Address: **No: 340, Taksim Square, Şişli, Istanbul**
  Phone: **+90 212 311 2000**
  This private hospital offers advanced healthcare facilities and is one of the top medical institutions in Istanbul.
- **Florence Nightingale Hospital**
  Address: **Mecidiyeköy, Istanbul**

Phone: **+90 212 320 2000**

Known for its high standards, this hospital provides both emergency and elective services.

- **Istanbul Medical Center (Istanbul Tıp Merkezi)**
  Address: **Büyükdere Caddesi 173, Levent, Istanbul**
  Phone: **+90 212 385 1000**

  This hospital offers a wide range of medical services, including emergency care.

Pharmacies:

Pharmacies in Istanbul are easy to find. Many are open late, and some even operate 24/7. In case of a medical issue that doesn't require an emergency room visit, you can visit a pharmacy for advice or over-the-counter medication. Pharmacies with a **"24 Saat Açık" (24-hour open)** sign are especially helpful for late-night needs.

Tourist Police:

Istanbul has a **Tourist Police** force, specifically designed to assist visitors with any issues or emergencies related to tourism. If you encounter a problem, you can reach them at **+90 212 527 4507**.

Transportation In Istanbul

Public Transportation

Istanbul has a well-developed public transportation system that includes buses, trains, trams, ferries, and metro lines. These are all convenient and affordable options for getting around the city.

Buses

Istanbul's bus network is extensive, covering almost every area of the city. Buses are a reliable way to travel, especially for areas that are not served by the metro or tram. Buses are often crowded during peak hours, so it's a good idea to plan your trips accordingly.

To use the bus, you'll need an **Istanbulkart**, a rechargeable travel card that works on almost all forms of public transportation in the city, including buses. Simply tap the card on the bus's card reader to board.

- **Bus Stops:** Buses in Istanbul stop at designated bus stations, which are easy to find across the city.
- **Schedules:** Buses generally run from early morning to late at night. Some routes even operate 24 hours a day, especially those in major areas.
- **Travel Tips:** During rush hours, buses can get very crowded, so try to plan your travel during off-peak times for a more comfortable ride.

Trams

Istanbul's tram system is another convenient and scenic way to travel, especially in tourist-friendly areas. The **T1 Tram Line** is particularly useful, as it connects major tourist spots like **Sultanahmet** (home to the Blue Mosque and Hagia Sophia) to **Kabataş**, where you can switch to ferries and other forms of transport.

- **Tram Stops:** Trams stop at stations along the route, and stops are clearly marked with signs.
- **Schedules:** Trams run frequently, and the system is very punctual, usually from around 6:00 AM to midnight.

- **Travel Tips:** Trams are popular with tourists, so they can be crowded at times, especially in the city center. During busy hours, be prepared for some wait time.

Metro

The Istanbul Metro is a fast and reliable way to get around the city, especially for long distances. The metro lines connect key neighborhoods and business districts. The **M2 Metro Line** runs through **Taksim** and connects with other lines, including the M1A and M4 lines.

- **Metro Stations:** The metro stations are located underground and are marked with clear signs, making it easy for travelers to find them.
- **Schedules:** The metro runs from around 6:00 AM until midnight, and some lines even operate later during the weekends.
- **Travel Tips:** The metro is usually not as crowded as buses or trams, making it a good choice for avoiding rush-hour congestion.

Ferries

Istanbul is divided by the **Bosphorus Strait**, so ferries are an essential part of the city's transportation network. Ferries are not only a practical way to travel between the European and Asian sides of the city, but they also offer stunning views of Istanbul from the water.

- **Ferry Stops:** Major ferry stops include **Eminönü** (European side), **Kabataş** (European side), **Kadıköy** (Asian side), and **Üsküdar** (Asian side).
- **Schedules:** Ferries run throughout the day, with more frequent departures during rush hours. The ride usually takes about 20 minutes between the two sides of the city.
- **Travel Tips:** Ferries can be a relaxing and scenic way to get from one side of Istanbul to the other, and they are often less crowded than other forms of public transport.

Jeepneys (Dolmuş)

While not as common in Istanbul as in some other parts of the world, there are shared taxis called **Dolmuş** or jeepneys that travel along fixed routes. These are small minibuses or vans that pick up passengers along their route and are a good option for traveling short distances or to places not easily accessible by other forms of transport.

- **Stops:** Dolmuşes pick up passengers at designated stops, usually near major streets or transportation hubs.
- **Fares:** The fare is usually very affordable and based on the distance traveled.
- **Travel Tips:** Dolmuşes are usually faster than buses but can be crowded, especially during peak hours.

Taxis And Ride-sharing Services

Taxis

Taxis in Istanbul are easy to find and are a popular way to travel around the city. Most taxis are yellow and can be hailed on the street, or you can book them by phone or through a mobile app.

- **Taxis Fare:** Taxis in Istanbul charge based on distance traveled, and there is a standard starting fare plus additional charges per kilometer. Always ensure the driver uses the meter, or agree on a fare before starting your journey to avoid any misunderstandings.
- **Taxi Stops:** Taxis can be found at designated taxi stands or hailed from the street. It's often more convenient to use an app to call a taxi if you're in a less busy area.

- **Travel Tips:** Taxi drivers may not always speak English, so it's helpful to have your destination written down in Turkish. Some taxis may also charge extra for luggage, so be aware of any additional fees.

Ride-Sharing Services

In addition to traditional taxis, ride-sharing services like **Uber** and **BiTaksi** (a local app) are available in Istanbul. These apps allow you to book a ride directly from your phone, with the price calculated based on the distance and time of day.

- **Fare Estimate:** The apps provide an estimate of the fare before you confirm your booking, so you know what to expect.
- **Travel Tips:** Ride-sharing services are often more convenient and sometimes cheaper than traditional taxis, especially for short trips.

Car Rentals

Renting a car in Istanbul is not the most popular option for most travelers because traffic can be heavy, and parking can be difficult to find, especially in central areas. However, if you prefer the flexibility of driving, car rental is available.

- **Car Rental Companies:** International car rental companies like **Avis**, **Europcar**, and **Hertz** operate in

Istanbul, and there are also local agencies where you can rent a car.

- **Driving in Istanbul:** Traffic in Istanbul can be challenging, particularly in the city center. Be prepared for congested roads, especially during rush hours (7:30 AM - 9:00 AM and 5:30 PM - 7:30 PM). Parking is limited, and some areas require paid parking.
- **Travel Tips:** If you're not familiar with the city's traffic patterns, using public transportation or taxis is a better option. However, renting a car is a good choice if you're planning to explore neighborhoods outside the city center.

Bicycles And Walking

Walking

Istanbul's neighborhoods are best explored on foot. Many of the city's main attractions are within walking distance of each other, especially in the Sultanahmet district. Walking is a great way to experience the city's history and culture up close.

- **Pedestrian Zones:** Istanbul has many pedestrian zones, particularly in the historic areas and shopping districts. These are safe and pleasant for walking.
- **Travel Tips:** Wear comfortable shoes because Istanbul's streets can be uneven and steep in some areas.

Bicycles

While Istanbul does not have a vast network of bike lanes, there are a few areas where cycling is possible. In recent years, the city has been making efforts to improve cycling infrastructure, particularly along the **Bosphorus** coast and in parks.

- **Bike Rentals:** There are a few places where you can rent bikes, and some bike-sharing systems are also available in certain parts of the city.
- **Travel Tips:** Be cautious when cycling in busy areas like **Taksim Square** or **Sultanahmet**, where traffic can be dense.

Top Tourist Attractions In Istanbul

1. Hagia Sophia (Ayasofya)

One of Istanbul's most famous landmarks, the Hagia Sophia has served as a church, mosque, and now a museum. Known for its massive dome, intricate mosaics, and rich history, this building represents the merging of Christianity and Islam. Whether you're there to admire the art, history, or architecture, it's an experience you won't forget.

- **Address:** Sultanahmet Square, Sultanahmet, 34122 Istanbul, Turkey
- **Phone Number:** +90 212 522 1750

2. Topkapi Palace (Topkapı Sarayı)

Topkapi Palace was once the residence of Ottoman sultans. This grand palace complex includes beautiful courtyards, impressive rooms, and museums showcasing the wealth and history of the Ottoman Empire. The **Harem**, the private section of the palace, is a popular area to visit. You'll also get a glimpse of the sacred relics of the Prophet Muhammad, housed in one of the palace's exhibits.

- **Address:** Cankurtaran, 34122 Fatih/Istanbul, Turkey
- **Phone Number:** +90 212 512 0480

3. Blue Mosque (Sultanahmet Camii)

The **Blue Mosque** is one of Istanbul's most iconic buildings. Built in the early 1600s, it's known for its impressive blue tiles that adorn its interior. It's still an active mosque, so visitors are asked to dress modestly. It's a place of peace, with stunning courtyards and a serene atmosphere.

- **Address:** Sultanahmet, 34122 Fatih/Istanbul, Turkey
- **Phone Number:** +90 212 458 1254

4. Basilica Cistern (Yerebatan Sarnıcı)

Hidden beneath the streets of Sultanahmet, the **Basilica Cistern** is an ancient underground water reservoir. It was built in the 6th century by the Byzantine Emperor Justinian to provide water to the Great Palace of Constantinople. The cistern is famous for its row of massive columns, with some even adorned with Medusa heads. The cool, dark atmosphere makes for a unique and slightly eerie experience.

- **Address:** Alemdar Mahallesi, Yerebatan Cd. No:13, 34110 Fatih/Istanbul, Turkey
- **Phone Number:** +90 212 522 1259

5. Galata Tower (Galata Kulesi)

The **Galata Tower** offers one of the best panoramic views of Istanbul. Located in the Galata district, this medieval stone tower is a great place to take in views of the Golden Horn, Bosphorus, and old Istanbul. There is also a restaurant and café at the top, where you can relax while enjoying the view.

- **Address:** Bereketzade, Galata Kulesi, 34421 Beyoğlu/Istanbul, Turkey
- **Phone Number:** +90 212 293 8133

6. Grand Bazaar (Kapalı Çarşı)

The **Grand Bazaar** is one of the largest and oldest covered markets in the world. With over 4,000 shops, you can find anything from jewelry and textiles to spices and souvenirs. It's a must-visit for anyone wanting to experience Istanbul's vibrant market culture. Be ready to haggle to get the best deals!

- **Address:** Beyazıt, 34126 Fatih/Istanbul, Turkey
- **Phone Number:** +90 212 519 1243
- **Opening Hours:** 9:00 AM – 7:00 PM (closed on Sundays)

7. Spice Bazaar (Mısır Çarşısı)

If you want to experience a different kind of market, the **Spice Bazaar** is the place to go. Filled with vibrant colors and fragrant smells, this market specializes in spices, herbs, dried fruits, nuts, and sweets. It's a fantastic spot to buy local treats like Turkish delight or baklava.

- **Address:** Rüstem Paşa, 34116 Fatih/Istanbul, Turkey
- **Phone Number:** +90 212 511 2880
- **Opening Hours:** 9:00 AM – 7:00 PM (closed on Sundays)

8. Süleymaniye Mosque (Süleymaniye Camii)

The **Süleymaniye Mosque** is one of the largest and most beautiful mosques in Istanbul. Designed by the famous architect

Mimar Sinan in the 16th century, it's known for its stunning architecture, serene courtyards, and breathtaking views of the city. It's a peaceful place to visit and a great example of Ottoman architecture.

- **Address:** Süleymaniye, 34116 Fatih/Istanbul, Turkey
- **Phone Number:** +90 212 518 1319
- **Opening Hours:** 9:00 AM – 6:00 PM (closed during prayer times)

9. Dolmabahçe Palace (Dolmabahçe Sarayı)

Once the administrative center of the Ottoman Empire, the **Dolmabahçe Palace** is a beautiful blend of European and Ottoman architectural styles. With its extravagant rooms, crystal chandeliers, and a large collection of art, it gives visitors a glimpse into the luxurious life of the sultans. Don't miss the chance to see the famous **Crystal Staircase** and the **Atatürk Room**, where the founder of modern Turkey, Mustafa Kemal Atatürk, passed away.

- **Address:** Vişnezade, Dolmabahçe Cd., 34357 Beşiktaş/Istanbul, Turkey
- **Phone Number:** +90 212 236 9000
- **Opening Hours:** 9:00 AM – 4:00 PM (closed on Mondays)

10. Bosphorus Cruise

A **Bosphorus Cruise** is a must-do for anyone visiting Istanbul. It offers a chance to sail between the European and Asian sides of the city, giving you a beautiful view of the city's landmarks like the **Dolmabahçe Palace**, **Rumeli Fortress**, and the **Maiden's Tower**. You can opt for a short, scenic ferry ride or a longer cruise that goes all the way up to the Black Sea.

- **Address:** Multiple departure points, including **Eminönü, Kabataş,** and **Üsküdar.**
- **Phone Number:** Varies by ferry operator (one popular operator is **Şehir Hatları**: +90 212 444 9595)
- **Opening Hours:** Varies by operator (typically 9:00 AM – 7:00 PM)

Accommodation In Istanbul

Luxury Resorts

Four Seasons Hotel Istanbul at Sultanahmet

This 5-star hotel is located right in the heart of the historic district, just steps away from the Hagia Sophia and the Blue Mosque. With its blend of modern luxury and Ottoman-inspired design, the hotel offers a serene atmosphere, elegant rooms, and top-notch facilities, including a spa, fine dining, and a rooftop terrace with stunning views of the Bosphorus.

- **Address:** Tevkifhane Sokak No:1, Sultanahmet, 34110 Istanbul, Turkey
- **Phone Number:** +90 212 402 3000

Ciragan Palace Kempinski Istanbul

Housed in an Ottoman palace on the shores of the Bosphorus, this luxurious resort is known for its royal charm and extensive facilities. Ciragan Palace boasts spacious rooms, beautiful gardens, an outdoor pool, and a famous restaurant with stunning Bosphorus views.

- **Address:** Çırağan Caddesi 32, Beşiktaş, 34349 Istanbul, Turkey
- **Phone Number:** +90 212 326 4646

The Ritz-Carlton, Istanbul

Set along the Bosphorus, The Ritz-Carlton offers a sophisticated stay with exquisite rooms, an exceptional spa, and a wide range of dining options. Guests can relax by the pool or enjoy the stunning views of the Bosphorus from the rooftop terrace.

- **Address:** Ahmet Adnan Saygun Caddesi No: 6, 34353 Istanbul, Turkey
- **Phone Number:** +90 212 334 4444

Shangri-La Bosphorus, Istanbul

This luxury hotel offers magnificent views of the Bosphorus, elegant rooms, and world-class amenities. With its spa, Michelin-starred restaurant, and easy access to Istanbul's key attractions, Shangri-La is an excellent choice for those seeking high-end luxury.

- **Address:** Sinanpaşa Mahallesi, Hayrettin İskelesi Sokak No:1, Beşiktaş, 34353 Istanbul, Turkey
- **Phone Number:** +90 212 275 8888

Swissotel The Bosphorus Istanbul

Offering stunning views of the Bosphorus and lush gardens, this luxury resort features spacious rooms, a spa, and multiple dining options. It's located close to major cultural sites like Dolmabahçe Palace and Taksim Square.

- **Address:** Vişnezade, South Entrance, 34357 Istanbul, Turkey
- **Phone Number:** +90 212 326 1100

Budget-Friendly Hotels

Hotel Amira Istanbul

Located in the Sultanahmet district, this budget hotel offers clean and comfortable rooms with free breakfast. It's within walking distance to the major attractions like the Blue Mosque, Hagia Sophia, and Topkapi Palace, making it an excellent option for sightseeing.

- **Address:** Kucuk Ayasofya Mahallesi, Kadirga Liman Cd. No: 14, Sultanahmet, 34122 Istanbul, Turkey
- **Phone Number:** +90 212 516 4874

The Sultan Hotel

Offering budget-friendly rooms in a prime location, this hotel is close to major historical landmarks. It's a simple yet comfortable choice for travelers who want to explore Istanbul without spending a fortune.

- **Address:** Cankurtaran Mahallesi, Akbıyık Caddesi No: 16, Sultanahmet, 34122 Istanbul, Turkey
- **Phone Number:** +90 212 458 1849

Cheers Hostel

If you're traveling solo or with friends, Cheers Hostel offers affordable dormitory-style accommodations with a great social atmosphere. Located in the heart of Sultanahmet, it's perfect for travelers who want to meet others and explore the city on a budget.

- **Address:** Cankurtaran Mahallesi, Akbıyık Caddesi No: 28, Sultanahmet, 34122 Istanbul, Turkey
- **Phone Number:** +90 212 516 2676

Pera Capitol Hotel

This 3-star hotel is in the vibrant Beyoğlu district, offering great value for money. It's close to Taksim Square, Istiklal Avenue, and many other attractions. The rooms are simple, clean, and well-maintained, perfect for budget-conscious travelers.

- **Address:** Kocatepe Mahallesi, Sehit Muhtar Cd. No: 37, Beyoğlu, 34437 Istanbul, Turkey
- **Phone Number:** +90 212 243 5858

Hotel Peninsula

A great value hotel located in Sultanahmet, this hotel offers basic amenities with a convenient location near top tourist sites like the Grand Bazaar and the Blue Mosque. It's perfect for travelers who want to keep their expenses low but still stay close to the action.

- **Address:** Kucuk Ayasofya Mahallesi, Sehit Mehmet Pasa Yokusu No: 28, Sultanahmet, 34122 Istanbul, Turkey
- **Phone Number:** +90 212 518 6300

Boutique Guesthouses

The Byzantium Hotel & Suites

Located in Sultanahmet, this boutique hotel combines Ottoman-style architecture with modern comforts. Guests can enjoy stylish rooms, personalized service, and easy access to major attractions.

- **Address:** Cankurtaran Mahallesi, Akbıyık Caddesi No: 46, Sultanahmet, 34122 Istanbul, Turkey
- **Phone Number:** +90 212 516 7280

Hotel Niles

This boutique hotel in Beyoğlu offers a unique experience with its rooftop terrace, cozy atmosphere, and stylish rooms. Guests can enjoy a free breakfast and explore nearby attractions such as Istiklal Avenue and Taksim Square.

- **Address:** Kocatepe Mahallesi, Yeniçeri Caddesi No: 7, Beyoğlu, 34437 Istanbul, Turkey
- **Phone Number:** +90 212 292 8606

Karaköy Rooms

A stylish boutique hotel located in the trendy Karaköy area,

Karaköy Rooms offers chic rooms with modern decor and excellent service. The hotel is close to the Galata Tower and other landmarks, perfect for travelers seeking a more personalized experience.

- **Address:** Kemankeş Karamustafa Paşa Mahallesi, Karaköy Cd. No: 16, Beyoğlu, 34425 Istanbul, Turkey
- **Phone Number:** +90 212 243 3724

Zeynep Sultan Hotel

This boutique hotel is located in Sultanahmet and offers guests a blend of traditional and modern Turkish design. With personalized service and a prime location near the major historic sites, it's an excellent choice for travelers looking for a more local experience.

- **Address:** Cankurtaran Mahallesi, Zeynep Sultan Camii Sokak No: 3, Sultanahmet, 34122 Istanbul, Turkey
- **Phone Number:** +90 212 458 0510

The House Hotel Bosphorus

A boutique hotel with a rich history, located right on the Bosphorus. The House Hotel offers a luxurious stay with personalized service, elegant rooms, and a beautiful setting, perfect for those who want a boutique experience with a great view.

- **Address:** Kuruçeşme Mahallesi, Bebek Yoku

Unique Stays

The Marmara Taksim

Located at Taksim Square, The Marmara offers a unique stay experience with a blend of modern luxury and historical significance. Its rooftop terrace offers panoramic views of the Bosphorus and the Golden Horn, providing a unique vantage point of the city's beauty.

- **Address:** Taksim Square, Beyoğlu, 34437 Istanbul, Turkey
- **Phone Number:** +90 212 313 3000

Cihangir Palace Hotel

A beautifully restored mansion offering a glimpse into Istanbul's past, this boutique hotel is located in the artsy Cihangir district. The rooms are uniquely designed, offering a blend of Ottoman style with modern amenities. Staying here gives guests a taste of Istanbul's history with the comfort of modern luxury.

- **Address:** Cihangir Mahallesi, Cihangir Yokuşu No: 24, Beyoğlu, 34433 Istanbul, Turkey
- **Phone Number:** +90 212 249 4102

House Hotel Galatasaray

A unique stay in a historical building, House Hotel Galatasaray combines modern design with the building's rich history. Located in the lively Beyoğlu district, it's a great base for exploring Istanbul's art scene, cafes, and boutique stores.

- **Address:** İstiklal Caddesi No: 29, Beyoğlu, 34433 Istanbul, Turkey

- **Phone Number:** +90 212 293 4242

Madanos Boutique Hotel

This unique hotel is located in a historic building in the Sultanahmet district and offers a cozy, home-like atmosphere. The hotel's décor reflects a mix of traditional and contemporary Turkish design, with each room offering a unique touch. It's perfect for visitors who want to experience the traditional charm of Istanbul.

- **Address:** Cankurtaran Mahallesi, Akbıyık Caddesi No: 45, Sultanahmet, 34122 Istanbul, Turkey
- **Phone Number:** +90 212 518 2525

Karaköy Port Hotel

A modern boutique hotel located in the vibrant Karaköy area, this unique stay combines stylish interiors with the lively atmosphere of the district. With beautiful views of the Golden Horn and a great location for exploring the trendy cafes, restaurants, and galleries of Karaköy, it's a fantastic option for those seeking something a little different.

- **Address:** Kemankeş Karamustafa Paşa Mahallesi, Karaköy Cd. No: 51, Beyoğlu, 34425 Istanbul, Turkey
- **Phone Number:** +90 212 249 7878

Top Recommended Accommodation

The Ritz-Carlton Istanbul

For those seeking luxury and exceptional service, The Ritz-Carlton is one of Istanbul's best hotels. Situated in the heart of Istanbul, it offers an outstanding spa, Michelin-starred dining, and magnificent views.

- **Address:** Ahmet Adnan Saygun Caddesi No: 6, 34353 Istanbul, Turkey
- **Phone Number:** +90 212 334 4444

Sirkeci Mansion Hotel

Located in the historical Sirkeci area, this boutique hotel offers a unique experience with traditional Turkish hospitality. Its location is perfect for those who want to explore Istanbul's old town, and the hotel offers cozy rooms and excellent service.

- **Address:** Sirkeci, 3, Taya Hatun Sokak, 34110 Istanbul, Turkey
- **Phone Number:** +90 212 520 8010

Radisson Blu Hotel, Istanbul Pera

This hotel is situated in the historic Pera district, offering views of the Golden Horn. It combines modern comforts with old-world charm and offers a wide range of dining options, a spa, and great service.

- **Address:** Tepebaşı, Mesrutiyet Caddesi 55, Beyoğlu, 34430 Istanbul, Turkey
- **Phone Number:** +90 212 377 7171

Mövenpick Hotel Istanbul

Located in the upscale Levent district, Mövenpick offers excellent service and a range of luxurious amenities. It's perfect for business travelers or those wanting a quieter stay while still being close to Istanbul's commercial areas.

- **Address:** Büyükdere Caddesi No: 1, Levent, 34330 Istanbul, Turkey
- **Phone Number:** +90 212 319 2929

Choosing The Right Accommodation For You

- **For Luxury:** If you're looking to indulge, go for the high-end resorts and luxury hotels located near iconic landmarks, like the Four Seasons or Ciragan Palace. These offer top-tier services and are perfect for those seeking comfort and style.
- **For Budget Travel:** If you're traveling on a budget, opt for smaller, budget-friendly hotels like Hotel Amira or Cheers Hostel. These accommodations provide good service at affordable rates while still being close to major attractions.
- **For Boutique Experiences:** If you enjoy unique, personalized experiences, boutique guesthouses like The Byzantium Hotel or Zeynep Sultan Hotel offer charming stays with a local touch.
- **For Unique Stays:** For something different, consider staying in a historical mansion or even a houseboat in places like Karaköy Port Hotel or House Hotel Bosphorus.
- **Location Matters:** Choose your accommodation based on proximity to the attractions you plan to visit. Staying in Sultanahmet puts you close to the historical sites, while Taksim and Beyoğlu are better for shopping and nightlife.

Booking Tips And Tricks

- **Book in Advance:** Istanbul is a popular tourist destination, and the best accommodations fill up quickly, especially during peak seasons. Book your stay as early as possible to secure the best rates.
- **Use Booking Websites:** Platforms like Booking.com, Airbnb, and Agoda often offer competitive prices and reviews that can help you make an informed decision.
- **Check Cancellation Policies:** Ensure you are aware of cancellation policies, especially during uncertain times, so you can make changes to your booking if needed.
- **Look for Deals:** Keep an eye out for promotions, discounts, and package deals that may include breakfast or guided tours, which can help you save money.
- **Consider Local Transportation:** If you plan to use public transport, choose accommodations near tram or metro stations to make your stay more convenient and affordable.
- **Read Reviews:** Always check guest reviews to get an honest opinion on the quality of service, cleanliness, and location.
- **Ask for Special Requests:** If you have any special requirements (e.g., a late check-in, early check-out, or specific room preference), contact the hotel beforehand to ensure your needs are met.

Dining And Nightlife In Istanbul

Local Cuisine

- **Kebabs**

  One of the most iconic dishes in Turkish cuisine, kebabs are grilled meat, often served with rice, vegetables, and flatbread. There are many types of kebabs, including Adana (spicy minced meat), Şiş (grilled chunks of meat), and Döner (meat cooked on a vertical rotisserie).

- **Baklava**

  For dessert, baklava is a must-try. It's a sweet pastry made of thin layers of dough, filled with chopped nuts (usually pistachios or walnuts) and sweetened with syrup or honey. It's crunchy, sticky, and delicious.

- **Meze**

  A variety of small dishes served before the main course, meze is the Turkish version of appetizers. You'll find a mix of cold and hot dishes like hummus, baba ghanoush, muhammara (spicy red pepper dip), and fried cheese. It's perfect for sharing with friends.

- **Pide**

  Often referred to as Turkish pizza, pide is a flatbread topped with cheese, minced meat, vegetables, and herbs. It's baked in a wood-fired oven and is crispy around the edges.

- **Simit**

  A type of sesame-crusted bread, simit is a popular snack in Istanbul. Often enjoyed with tea, it's sold by street vendors throughout the city and is an ideal breakfast or snack.

Popular Restaurants

Nusr-Et Steakhouse

Famous for its high-quality steaks and celebrity chef Nusret Gökçe (also known as Salt Bae), Nusr-Et has become a sensation in Istanbul. The restaurant offers a variety of meat cuts, all cooked to perfection.

- **Address**: Kanyon AVM, Büyükdere Caddesi No: 185, 34394 Levent, Istanbul.
- **Phone**: +90 212 353 2838
- **Opening Hours**: Monday to Sunday, 12:00 PM - 12:00 AM.

Çiya Sofrası

Located on the Asian side of Istanbul, Çiya Sofrası offers a deep dive into traditional Anatolian dishes. It's well-known for its wide variety of regional recipes, including stews, pilafs, and meze.

- **Address**: Guneslibahce Sokak No: 43, Kadıköy, 34710 Istanbul.
- **Phone**: +90 216 330 3190
- **Opening Hours**: Monday to Sunday, 11:00 AM - 10:00 PM.

Mikla Restaurant

Situated on the top floor of the Marmara Pera Hotel, Mikla offers stunning views of Istanbul. It serves a contemporary Turkish menu, combining traditional flavors with modern techniques. The restaurant is also known for its excellent wine list.

- **Address**: The Marmara Pera Hotel, Meşrutiyet Caddesi No: 15, Beyoğlu, Istanbul.
- **Phone**: +90 212 293 5656
- **Opening Hours**: Monday to Sunday, 6:00 PM - 12:00 AM.

Beyti Restaurant

Located in the Florya district, Beyti is known for its high-quality Turkish cuisine, especially its kebabs. The restaurant has been serving Turkish specialties since 1945 and is loved by both locals and tourists.

- **Address**: Orman Caddesi No: 8, Florya, 34153 Bakirkoy, Istanbul.
- **Phone**: +90 212 663 8787
- **Opening Hours**: Monday to Sunday, 12:00 PM - 12:00 AM.

Street Food

- **Simit**

  As mentioned earlier, simit is a sesame-crusted bread that's sold by street vendors throughout Istanbul. You can find simit vendors on almost every corner, and it's often eaten with a glass of Turkish tea.
- **Köfte**

  Turkish meatballs, or köfte, are often served in a sandwich with fresh vegetables and a side of yogurt or salad. These are common street foods, especially in busy districts like Taksim and Kadıköy.

- **Balık Ekmek (Fish Sandwich)**

  A popular street food near the Galata Bridge, balık ekmek is a fish sandwich typically made with grilled mackerel, onions, lettuce, and served in a crusty bread roll. It's often enjoyed by locals and visitors alike while overlooking the Bosphorus.

- **Lahmacun**

  Often referred to as Turkish pizza, lahmacun is a thin, crispy flatbread topped with a mixture of minced meat, vegetables, and spices. It's rolled up and eaten with a side of fresh herbs and lemon.

- **Dondurma (Turkish Ice Cream)**

  Turkish ice cream, or dondurma, is thicker and chewier than regular ice cream, thanks to the use of salep (a flour made from orchids). Vendors often entertain tourists with their playful tricks while serving up a cone of this delicious ice cream.

Cafés And Bakeries

Pelit Patisserie

Pelit is one of Istanbul's oldest and most beloved patisseries. Known for its rich, delicious chocolates, cakes, and pastries, it has become a favorite stop for anyone with a sweet tooth. Pelit also offers Turkish delights and other regional desserts.

- **Address**: Bağdat Caddesi No: 370, Kadıköy, 34744 Istanbul.
- **Phone**: +90 216 573 2444
- **Opening Hours**: Monday to Sunday, 8:00 AM - 12:00 AM.

Çınaraltı Çay Bahçesi

Located along the Bosphorus in the neighborhood of Çengelköy, this café offers stunning views and a relaxing atmosphere. The café is famous for its tea (çay) served in traditional tulip-shaped glasses, perfect for a peaceful moment overlooking the water. It also offers a selection of small snacks and pastries.

- **Address**: Çengelköy, İsmail Ağa Caddesi No: 2, Üsküdar, Istanbul.
- **Phone**: +90 216 386 5757
- **Opening Hours**: Monday to Sunday, 8:00 AM - 12:00 AM.

Mendel's Bakery

A cozy spot for anyone who loves freshly baked bread, Mendel's Bakery is well-known for its European-style pastries, breads, and cakes. It's a great place to grab breakfast or brunch, with plenty of seating to enjoy a leisurely meal.

- **Address**: Arnavutköy, Abdülezelpaşa Caddesi No: 28, Beşiktaş, 34345 Istanbul.
- **Phone**: +90 212 261 3060

- **Opening Hours**: Monday to Sunday, 7:00 AM - 8:00 PM.

Bars And Nightclubs

360 Istanbul

 Offering one of the best panoramic views of the city, 360 Istanbul is a trendy rooftop bar and restaurant located in the heart of Beyoğlu. The bar offers a wide selection of cocktails, as well as a great dining menu. It's perfect for a night out with friends or a romantic evening.

- **Address**: İstiklal Caddesi No: 163, Beyoğlu, 34403 Istanbul.
- **Phone**: +90 212 251 1042

- **Opening Hours**: Monday to Sunday, 6:00 PM - 2:00 AM.

Babylon

One of Istanbul's most famous live music venues, Babylon hosts concerts by both local and international artists. The venue offers a mix of genres, including jazz, rock, and electronic music. It's an excellent place for music lovers to enjoy a lively night out.

- **Address**: Asmalı Mescit Mahallesi, Nevizade Caddesi No: 19, Beyoğlu, 34430 Istanbul.
- **Phone**: +90 212 252 0300
- **Opening Hours**: Monday to Sunday, 8:00 PM - 3:00 AM.

Reina

One of the most exclusive nightclubs in Istanbul, Reina offers a luxurious experience with international DJs, high-end service, and an incredible view of the Bosphorus. It's a favorite for those looking to dance the night away in style.

- **Address**: Ortaköy, Muallim Naci Caddesi No: 44, Beşiktaş, 34347 Istanbul.
- **Phone**: +90 212 263 6666
- **Opening Hours**: Friday to Saturday, 11:00 PM - 6:00 AM.

Nardis Jazz Club

For jazz enthusiasts, Nardis Jazz Club in the Galata area is a great place to enjoy live performances. The club hosts a variety of jazz artists and provides an intimate and cozy atmosphere, perfect for a relaxed night out.

- **Address**: Kuledibi, Galip Dede Caddesi No: 55, Beyoğlu, 34421 Istanbul.
- **Phone**: +90 212 292 8939
- **Opening Hours**: Monday to Sunday, 7:30 PM - 2:00 AM.

Night Markets

Kadıköy Market

Located on the Asian side, Kadıköy Market is open late into the evening, offering a mix of fresh produce, seafood, and unique local products. It's a great spot to experience the flavors of Istanbul and pick up some authentic goods.

- **Address**: Kadıköy, Caferağa Mahallesi, 34710 Istanbul.
- **Phone**: +90 216 346 7131
- **Opening Hours**: Monday to Sunday, 7:00 AM - 12:00 AM.

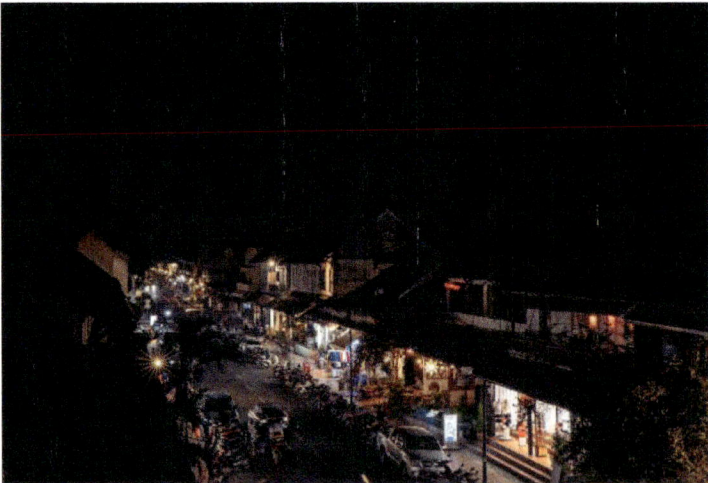

Eminönü Spice Bazaar

Open until late at night, the Spice Bazaar in Eminönü is a sensory experience. This historic market is filled with colorful stalls selling spices, sweets, dried fruits, and other unique items. It's the perfect place to wander around, sampling Turkish delights and other traditional treats.

- **Address**: Rüstem Paşa Mahallesi, Misir Çarşısı, 34116 Istanbul.
- **Phone**: +90 212 518 5310
- **Opening Hours**: Monday to Sunday, 9:00 AM - 11:00 PM.

Mısır Çarşısı (Egyptian Bazaar)

Also known as the Spice Bazaar, Mısır Çarşısı is a popular market in the heart of Istanbul. It's especially known for selling spices, herbs, and dried fruits. You can also find many street vendors offering delicious snacks like simit, roasted chestnuts, and baklava.

- **Address**: Rüstem Paşa Mahallesi, Misir Çarşısı, 34116 Istanbul.
- **Phone**: +90 212 518 5310
- **Opening Hours**: Monday to Sunday, 9:00 AM - 10:00 PM.

Shopping In Istanbul

Shopping Malls

Istinye Park Mall

 Istinye Park is one of Istanbul's most upscale malls, located in the Sarıyer district. It offers a wide range of luxury brands, including Gucci, Louis Vuitton, and Prada, as well as mid-range and high-street options. Besides shopping, Istinye Park also has a large food court with a variety of dining options, a cinema, and even a park with walking trails.

- **Address**: Pınar Mahallesi, Kemerburgaz Caddesi No: 22, Sarıyer, 34460 Istanbul.
- **Phone**: +90 212 345 4600
- **Opening Hours**: Monday to Sunday, 10:00 AM - 10:00 PM.

74

Cevahir Shopping Mall

One of the largest shopping malls in Istanbul, Cevahir Mall is located in Şişli and features a vast selection of shops, from popular international brands like Zara and Nike to local Turkish retailers. The mall also has a large entertainment section, including a bowling alley, cinema, and even an amusement park on the roof.

- **Address**: Büyükdere Caddesi No: 22, Şişli, 34360 Istanbul.
- **Phone**: +90 212 370 5600
- **Opening Hours**: Monday to Sunday, 10:00 AM - 10:00 PM.

Kanyon Mall

Kanyon is an open-air shopping mall that blends modern architecture with nature. Located in the Levent district, Kanyon is home to a variety of high-end brands, as well as mid-range options. The mall also offers an array of restaurants, a cinema, and cultural events throughout the year.

- **Address**: Büyükdere Caddesi No: 185, Levent, 34394 Istanbul.
- **Phone**: +90 212 353 5353
- **Opening Hours**: Monday to Sunday, 10:00 AM - 10:00 PM.

Forum Istanbul Shopping Mall

Forum Istanbul is a massive shopping complex located in the Bayrampaşa district. It features a wide range of international brands, as well as a variety of entertainment options. One of the mall's highlights is the Istanbul Aquarium, which is one of the largest aquariums in Europe, and LEGOLAND Discovery Centre, which is perfect for families with children.

- **Address**: Kocatepe Mahallesi, Paşa Caddesi No: 5, Bayrampaşa, 34035 Istanbul.
- **Phone**: +90 212 443 3700
- **Opening Hours**: Monday to Sunday, 10:00 AM - 10:00 PM.

Zorlu Center

Zorlu Center is another luxury shopping mall in Istanbul, located in Beşiktaş. It hosts high-end global brands such as Apple, Montblanc, and Burberry. Apart from shopping, Zorlu also has a performing arts center, fine dining restaurants, and a cinema, offering a complete cultural and shopping experience.

- **Address**: Levazım Mahallesi, Zorlu Center, Beşiktaş, 34340 Istanbul.
- **Phone**: +90 212 489 4000
- **Opening Hours**: Monday to Sunday, 10:00 AM - 10:00 PM.

Souvenir Shops

Grand Bazaar

One of the most famous landmarks in Istanbul, the Grand Bazaar (Kapalıçarşı) is a must-visit for souvenir shopping. The bazaar is filled with hundreds of shops selling everything from colorful carpets, jewelry, and ceramics to Turkish delight, spices, and antiques. The Grand Bazaar is a great place to haggle and find unique, handmade items.

- **Address**: Beyazıt, Kalpakçılar Caddesi, 34126 Istanbul.
- **Phone**: +90 212 520 7270
- **Opening Hours**: Monday to Saturday, 9:00 AM - 7:00 PM (Closed on Sundays).

Spice Bazaar (Mısır Çarşısı)

Located in the Eminönü district, the Spice Bazaar is famous for its colorful stalls that offer a variety of spices, herbs, teas, Turkish delight, dried fruits, and nuts. It's the perfect place to buy traditional ingredients or take home a pack of Turkish delight as a gift.

- **Address**: Rüstem Paşa Mahallesi, Misir Çarşısı, 34116 Istanbul.
- **Phone**: +90 212 518 5310
- **Opening Hours**: Monday to Saturday, 9:00 AM - 7:00 PM (Closed on Sundays).

Sultanahmet Square Souvenir Shops

Sultanahmet Square is the heart of Istanbul's tourist area, and you'll find plenty of souvenir shops here. From Turkish coffee sets and magnets to handcrafted jewelry, leather goods, and scarves, these shops sell a range of affordable souvenirs. Be sure to check out the shops along the streets leading up to the Blue Mosque and Hagia Sophia.

- **Address**: Sultanahmet, 34122 Istanbul.
- **Phone**: No specific phone number, as there are multiple stores in the area.
- **Opening Hours**: Varies by shop, typically 10:00 AM - 8:00 PM.

Arasta Bazaar

Located near the Blue Mosque in Sultanahmet, Arasta Bazaar is a quieter, more relaxed market compared to the Grand Bazaar. The shops here specialize in traditional Turkish crafts such as handwoven carpets, ceramics, textiles, and jewelry. It's a great place to shop for high-quality, unique souvenirs without the overwhelming crowds of the Grand Bazaar.

- **Address**: Sultanahmet, 34122 Istanbul.
- **Phone**: +90 212 517 0376
- **Opening Hours**: Monday to Saturday, 9:00 AM - 6:00 PM (Closed on Sundays).

Mısır Çarşısı (Egyptian Bazaar)

The Spice Bazaar is also known as the Egyptian Bazaar and is one of the oldest markets in Istanbul. Besides spices, you'll find plenty of Turkish sweets, nuts, and herbal teas. It's an excellent place to buy gifts like traditional Turkish copperware, glass lanterns, and handmade soaps.

- **Address**: Rüstem Paşa Mahallesi, Misir Çarşısı, 34116 Istanbul.
- **Phone**: +90 212 518 5310
- **Opening Hours**: Monday to Saturday, 9:00 AM - 7:00 PM (Closed on Sundays).

Çukurcuma Antique Shops

If you're looking for unique antiques or vintage items, Çukurcuma is the place to be. Located in the Beyoğlu district, this street is lined with antique shops selling everything from old furniture and glassware to vintage postcards, coins, and paintings.

It's a treasure trove for collectors and anyone who appreciates history.

- **Address**: Çukurcuma, Beyoğlu, 34425 Istanbul.
- **Phone**: No specific phone number, as there are multiple stores in the area.
- **Opening Hours**: Varies by shop, typically 10:00 AM - 7:00 PM.

Local Markets

Kadıköy Market

Located on the Asian side of Istanbul, Kadıköy Market is one of the city's oldest and most famous markets. It is a place where locals shop for everything from fresh fruit and vegetables to cheese, fish, and Turkish spices. Along with food, you'll find shops selling clothing, accessories, and homemade products. It's also a great spot to enjoy local street food like kumpir (stuffed baked potatoes) and simit (Turkish sesame bread).

- **Address**: Kadıköy, 34710 Istanbul (Near Kadıköy Ferry Terminal).
- **Phone**: +90 216 337 1130
- **Opening Hours**: Monday to Saturday, 9:00 AM - 7:00 PM (Closed on Sundays).

Fatih Market (Mahalle Pazarı)

Fatih Market is a lively, traditional market where locals come to shop for fresh produce, meat, fish, and flowers. The market is less touristy compared to others, giving visitors a chance to experience daily life in Istanbul. You'll find plenty of small shops selling clothes, household items, and textiles as well. It's a great place to purchase ingredients to take home or grab a quick snack.

- **Address**: Fatih, 34087 Istanbul.
- **Opening Hours**: Monday to Saturday, 9:00 AM - 6:00 PM (Closed on Sundays).

Beşiktaş Market

Beşiktaş is another lively district where locals shop for groceries, fish, meats, and traditional Turkish products. The market is surrounded by many small cafés and eateries, making it an excellent spot to stop for a quick bite while browsing the stalls.

The atmosphere is energetic and gives you a taste of everyday life in Istanbul.

- **Address**: Beşiktaş, 34353 Istanbul.
- **Opening Hours**: Monday to Saturday, 9:00 AM - 7:00 PM (Closed on Sundays).

Ortaköy Market

Ortaköy, located near the Bosphorus, is famous for its market, where you can find a mix of food, clothing, and handmade items. The market is popular for its antique and jewelry stalls, selling unique and high-quality products. It's also a great place to shop for souvenirs, especially artsy items like paintings, pottery, and handmade crafts.

- **Address**: Ortaköy, 34347 Istanbul.

- **Opening Hours**: Monday to Saturday, 9:00 AM - 6:00 PM (Closed on Sundays).

Luxury Boutiques

Beymen

Beymen is one of Turkey's leading luxury department stores, offering a curated selection of high-end fashion, jewelry, and home goods. With both international and Turkish designer brands, Beymen provides a premium shopping experience. The store is located in Zorlu Center, which is known for its luxury offerings.

- **Address**: Zorlu Center, Levazım Mahallesi, Beşiktaş, 34340 Istanbul.
- **Phone**: +90 212 354 5900

- **Opening Hours**: Monday to Saturday, 10:00 AM - 10:00 PM, Sunday, 12:00 PM - 8:00 PM.

Vakko

Vakko is a well-known Turkish luxury brand, offering fashion, accessories, and home décor. The store has an elegant atmosphere, and its collections are both sophisticated and stylish. Vakko also has a selection of high-end fabrics and Turkish-made textiles that make for great souvenirs.

- **Address**: Teşvikiye Caddesi No: 7/1, Nişantaşı, 34365 Istanbul.
- **Phone**: +90 212 291 9292
- **Opening Hours**: Monday to Saturday, 10:00 AM - 7:00 PM, Sunday Closed.

Louis Vuitton Istanbul

The Louis Vuitton boutique in Istanbul is located in the luxury Zorlu Center mall. This high-end store offers the brand's iconic leather goods, clothing, shoes, and accessories. The store is well-designed and offers a luxury shopping experience with attentive customer service.

- **Address**: Zorlu Center, Levazım Mahallesi, Beşiktaş, 34340 Istanbul.
- **Phone**: +90 212 963 6222
- **Opening Hours**: Monday to Saturday, 10:00 AM - 10:00 PM, Sunday, 12:00 PM - 8:00 PM.

Chanel Istanbul

The Chanel store in Istanbul offers the brand's luxurious clothing, handbags, jewelry, and cosmetics. Located in the Nişantaşı area, this boutique carries the latest collections and provides a sophisticated shopping experience for those seeking premium fashion.

- **Address**: Nişantaşı, Maçka Caddesi No: 55, 34367 Istanbul.
- **Phone**: +90 212 291 8777
- **Opening Hours**: Monday to Saturday, 10:00 AM - 7:00 PM, Sunday Closed.

Unique Finds

Çukurcuma Antique Shops

Located in the Beyoğlu district, Çukurcuma is known for its antique shops selling vintage items, including furniture, glassware, clocks, and collectibles. Many of the antiques have historical significance, making them excellent gifts or souvenirs. If you enjoy hunting for rare and unique items, this is the place to go.

- **Address**: Çukurcuma, Beyoğlu, 34425 Istanbul.
- **Phone**: No specific phone number, as it is an area with multiple shops.
- **Opening Hours**: Monday to Saturday, 10:00 AM - 6:00 PM (Individual shop hours may vary).

Pera Museum Gift Shop

The Pera Museum Gift Shop offers a unique selection of art-inspired souvenirs, including prints, books, and replicas of famous artworks. Located near the museum, this shop allows visitors to bring home items inspired by the museum's exhibitions. The store offers a variety of art-related products, making it a great stop for those interested in Istanbul's artistic heritage.

- **Address**: Meşrutiyet Caddesi No: 65, Tepebaşı, Beyoğlu, 34430 Istanbul.
- **Phone**: +90 212 334 9910
- **Opening Hours**: Tuesday to Saturday, 10:00 AM - 6:00 PM, Sunday, 12:00 PM - 6:00 PM, Monday Closed.

Grand Bazaar (Kapalıçarşı)

The Grand Bazaar is not only great for souvenirs, but it is also a place where you can find unique and rare items such as antiques, jewelry, carpets, and textiles. The hundreds of shops within the bazaar specialize in various goods, and it's an excellent place to haggle and find one-of-a-kind items. Whether it's a traditional hand-woven carpet or a beautiful antique, you'll find many items that reflect Turkey's rich history and culture.

- **Address**: Beyazıt, Kalpakçılar Caddesi, 34126 Istanbul.
- **Phone**: +90 212 520 7270
- **Opening Hours**: Monday to Saturday, 9:00 AM - 7:00 PM (Closed on Sundays).

Outdoor Activities

Parks And Green Spaces

Emirgan Park

Located on the European side, Emirgan Park is one of the largest and most famous parks in Istanbul. It features beautiful tulip gardens, walking paths, and peaceful ponds. It's an ideal place to enjoy a quiet afternoon, go for a jog, or simply relax by the water. During spring, the park hosts a famous tulip festival, attracting many visitors who come to see the vibrant flowers in full bloom.

- **Address**: Emirgan, 34467 Sarıyer, Istanbul.
- **Phone**: +90 212 323 0058
- **Opening Hours**: Open every day, 7:00 AM - 10:00 PM.

89

Gülhane Park

 Gülhane Park, located in the heart of Istanbul near the Topkapi Palace, is one of the city's oldest and most popular parks. It is a perfect place for a leisurely walk, with tree-lined paths, beautiful gardens, and plenty of benches to sit and relax. You can enjoy the fresh air, watch the local birds, and even grab a coffee from one of the nearby cafés.

- **Address**: Gülhane Park, Sultanahmet, 34112 Istanbul.
- **Phone**: No specific phone number.
- **Opening Hours**: Open every day, 7:00 AM - 10:00 PM.

Yıldız Park

 Yıldız Park is a large green area located near Beşiktaş. It's a lovely spot to escape the city's noise, offering many walking paths, scenic views, and peaceful areas for a picnic. The park also has two small palaces, Yıldız Palace and Malta Köşkü, where you can enjoy the beautiful architecture and surroundings. It's a great place to spend a relaxing afternoon.

- **Address**: Yıldız, 34349 Beşiktaş, Istanbul.
- **Phone**: +90 212 258 7667
- **Opening Hours**: Open every day, 7:00 AM - 10:00 PM.

Büyükçekmece Beach and Park

 Located on the western outskirts of Istanbul, Büyükçekmece is a large park and beach area where you can enjoy a day by the water. The park offers walking trails, playgrounds for children, and cafes along the coastline. The area is perfect for families, picnics, and those who want to relax by the sea.

- **Address**: Büyükçekmece, 34500 Istanbul.
- **Phone**: No specific phone number.
- **Opening Hours**: Open every day, 8:00 AM - 8:00 PM.

Water Activities

Bosphorus Cruise

A Bosphorus cruise is one of the best ways to see the city from a unique perspective. These boat tours take you along the Bosphorus Strait, offering views of Istanbul's stunning skyline, palaces, and bridges. You'll pass by famous landmarks such as the Dolmabahçe Palace and the Maiden's Tower, all while enjoying the cool breeze of the sea. There are both public and private tours available.

- **Address**: Embark at the Eminönü Ferry Terminal or Karaköy Pier.
- **Phone**: +90 212 444 7757

Kadıköy Beach

Kadıköy is a lively district on the Asian side of Istanbul that offers a small but popular beach area. It's a great spot to enjoy the sun, take a dip in the sea, or rent a paddleboard. While not as large as other beaches, it's a great place for a quick swim or just to relax by the water.

- **Address**: Kadıköy, 34710 Istanbul.
- **Phone**: No specific phone number.
- **Opening Hours**: Open every day, 9:00 AM - 6:00 PM (beach access may be limited in winter).

Marmara Sea Beaches

If you want to escape the city and enjoy a more tranquil environment, head to the Marmara Sea beaches located on the outskirts of Istanbul. The area around Silivri offers quiet beaches and a more relaxed atmosphere. You can rent sunbeds, enjoy beach sports, or simply enjoy the view of the sea.

- **Address**: Silivri, 34570 Istanbul.

Hiking And Nature Trails

Polonezköy Nature Park

Located on the Asian side, Polonezköy Nature Park is a peaceful area with hiking trails, forested areas, and picnic spots. The park offers a variety of paths for all levels of hikers. You can enjoy nature, wildlife, and even stop by one of the small local cafés for a rest.

- **Address**: Polonezköy, 34810 Istanbul.
- **Phone**: +90 216 460 1040
- **Opening Hours**: Open every day, 7:00 AM - 6:00 PM.

Belgrad Forest

Belgrad Forest is located on the European side of Istanbul and is one of the city's largest green areas. The forest has well-marked trails for walking, running, and cycling. It's a popular spot for locals who want to enjoy nature without leaving the city. The park also has several lakes and areas for picnics.

- **Address**: Belgrad Ormanı, 34450 Istanbul.
- **Phone**: No specific phone number.
- **Opening Hours**: Open every day, 7:00 AM - 7:00 PM.

Çatalca Hiking Trails

For a more rural hiking experience, head to Çatalca, located on the outskirts of Istanbul. This area offers long nature trails, providing visitors with scenic views of forests, meadows, and hills. It's perfect for a day trip from Istanbul if you're looking for a more secluded natural escape.

- **Address**: Çatalca, 34500 Istanbul.
- **Phone**: No specific phone number.
- **Opening Hours**: Open every day, 9:00 AM - 5:00 PM.

Sports And Recreation Centers

Istanbul Tennis Center

The Istanbul Tennis Center offers courts for both recreational and competitive players. Whether you're a beginner or an experienced player, you can book a court and enjoy a game with friends. The center also offers tennis lessons and has an indoor arena for year-round play.

- **Address**: Yeşilköy, Atatürk Caddesi, 34149 Istanbul.
- **Phone**: +90 212 663 4023
- **Opening Hours**: Monday to Sunday, 8:00 AM - 9:00 PM.

İstanbul Ice Skating Arena

The İstanbul Ice Skating Arena, located in the Kucukcekmece district, is a popular spot for ice skating enthusiasts. Whether you're a beginner or an expert, you can rent skates and enjoy a fun time on the ice. The arena also offers lessons for beginners and organizes ice hockey and figure skating events. It's a great place to visit with family or friends, especially during the colder months.

- **Address**: İkitelli, Atatürk Mah. 10. Yıl Cad. No:20, 34303, Küçükçekmece, Istanbul.
- **Phone**: +90 212 438 5400
- **Opening Hours**: Monday to Sunday, 10:00 AM - 10:00 PM.

Aqua Florya

Located by the Marmara Sea, Aqua Florya is a large shopping

mall that also has recreational facilities, including an indoor swimming pool and a bowling alley. It's perfect for a day of fun with family or friends, and after your swim or game, you can enjoy some shopping or a meal in one of the many restaurants at the mall.

- **Address**: Yeşilköy, Şenlikköy Mahallesi, Atatürk Cd. No:6, 34149 Bakırköy, Istanbul.
- **Phone**: +90 212 466 4200
- **Opening Hours**: Monday to Sunday, 10:00 AM - 10:00 PM.

Vialand (Istanbul) Theme Park and Sports Complex

Vialand is a popular amusement park and recreation center offering a range of activities. From thrilling rides to go-karting, there's something for everyone. The park also has a sports complex where you can play basketball, soccer, and other sports. It's an excellent choice for families looking for an action-packed day out.

- **Address**: Yeşilpınar, Sultançiftliği, 34065 Eyüp Sultan, Istanbul.
- **Phone**: +90 212 440 1000
- **Opening Hours**: Monday to Sunday, 10:00 AM - 7:00 PM (hours vary by season).

Cultural Experiences

Museums And Art Galleries

The Istanbul Museum of Modern Art (Istanbul Modern)

This museum is one of Turkey's leading contemporary art spaces. It showcases both Turkish and international artists, with exhibits spanning painting, sculpture, photography, and video art. The museum frequently hosts workshops, lectures, and screenings.

- **Address**: Meclis-i Mebusan Caddesi, Liman İşletmesi Sahası, Antrepo 4, Karaköy, Istanbul.
- **Phone**: +90 212 334 7300
- **Opening Hours**: Tuesday to Sunday, 10:00 AM - 6:00 PM (closed on Mondays).

97

Topkapi Palace Museum

A must-visit for those interested in Ottoman history, the Topkapi Palace was the residence of Ottoman sultans for almost 400 years. Today, it houses an impressive collection of Ottoman artifacts, including the famous Topkapi Dagger and the Spoonmaker's Diamond.

- **Address**: Cankurtaran Mahallesi, 34122 Fatih/Istanbul.
- **Phone**: +90 212 512 0480
- **Opening Hours**: Every day except Tuesdays, 9:00 AM - 6:00 PM.

Hagia Sophia Museum

Once a church, later a mosque, and now a museum, Hagia Sophia is one of the most famous landmarks in Istanbul. It's a stunning example of Byzantine architecture with an awe-inspiring interior, featuring mosaics, columns, and impressive domes.

- **Address**: Ayasofya Meydanı, Sultanahmet, 34122 Istanbul.
- **Phone**: +90 212 522 1750
- **Opening Hours**: Daily, 9:00 AM - 7:00 PM.

Pera Museum

This art museum is known for its collection of Orientalist art, as well as its temporary exhibitions of modern and contemporary art. The museum is housed in a beautifully restored historical building, and it also has a café offering a great view of the surrounding area.

- **Address**: Meşrutiyet Caddesi No: 65, Tepebaşı, Beyoğlu, Istanbul.
- **Phone**: +90 212 334 9900
- **Opening Hours**: Tuesday to Saturday, 10:00 AM - 7:00 PM (closed on Mondays).

Historical Sites

Basilica Cistern

This ancient underground water reservoir was built by the Byzantine Emperor Justinian I in the 6th century. It's an eerie and atmospheric site, with large columns and dim lighting. The most famous feature of the cistern is the Medusa head columns.

- **Address**: Yerebatan Caddesi 1, Sultanahmet, 34110 Istanbul.
- **Phone**: +90 212 522 1259
- **Opening Hours**: Daily, 9:00 AM - 6:30 PM.

Blue Mosque (Sultan Ahmed Mosque)

The Blue Mosque is one of Istanbul's most iconic landmarks, known for its blue-tiled interior and its six towering minarets. Visitors can admire the impressive architecture and the serene courtyard. The mosque is still in use for daily prayers, so it's important to dress modestly.

- **Address**: Sultanahmet, 34122 Istanbul.
- **Phone**: +90 212 458 1600
- **Opening Hours**: Daily, 9:00 AM - 6:00 PM (closed for prayer times).

Galata Tower

Offering some of the best panoramic views of Istanbul, Galata Tower is one of the city's oldest and most recognizable landmarks. The tower has served as a watchtower, a prison, and now a popular tourist attraction with a restaurant and viewing platform at the top.

- **Address**: Bereketzade Mahallesi, Galata Kulesi, 34421 Beyoğlu, Istanbul.
- **Phone**: +90 212 293 8180
- **Opening Hours**: Daily, 9:00 AM - 8:30 PM.

Chora Church (Kariye Museum)

Located a bit outside the city's main tourist areas, this stunning Byzantine church is famous for its remarkable mosaics and frescoes depicting scenes from the life of Christ. The church is a perfect example of Byzantine art and architecture.

- **Address**: Kariye Cami Sk. No: 16, Edirnekapı, 34087 Fatih/Istanbul.
- **Phone**: +90 212 631 9240
- **Opening Hours**: Tuesday to Sunday, 9:00 AM - 5:00 PM (closed on Mondays).

Traditional Festivals

Istanbul Tulip Festival

In April, Istanbul's parks and gardens come to life with colorful tulips. The Tulip Festival is a celebration of this beautiful flower, which was brought to the city from the Ottoman Empire. The festival includes activities for families, photography exhibitions, and garden tours.

- **When**: April.

Istanbul International Film Festival
Held every spring, this festival showcases films from around the world. It's a great opportunity for movie lovers to experience global cinema, with a focus on contemporary films from diverse cultures.

- **When**: April.

Ramadan and Eid Celebrations
During Ramadan, Istanbul takes on a festive atmosphere with special prayers, food markets, and cultural events. The most significant celebration is Eid al-Fitr, which marks the end of Ramadan. The city hosts concerts, religious ceremonies, and public feasts.

- **When**: April-May

Performing Arts And Theaters

State Opera and Ballet
The Istanbul State Opera and Ballet is a prestigious institution that offers regular performances of opera and ballet. You can enjoy

classic operas, contemporary ballet, and Turkish folk music performances.

- **Address**: Atatürk Caddesi, Harbiye, 34357 Şişli, Istanbul.
- **Phone**: +90 212 252 1557

Istanbul City Theaters

These state-run theaters feature a wide range of performances, from classical plays to modern works, often showcasing Turkish playwrights and international pieces. The city theaters have numerous locations across Istanbul, including the famous Harbiye Cemil Topuzlu Open-Air Theater.

- **Address**: Harbiye Cemil Topuzlu Parkı, 34367 Şişli, Istanbul.
- **Phone**: +90 212 293 5050

Beyoğlu Culture and Arts Foundation (BKM)

The BKM is one of the most popular venues in Istanbul for contemporary performances, from comedy to live concerts. It's a great place to see Turkish stand-up comedians, theater productions, and music events.

- **Address**: İstiklal Caddesi No: 119, Beyoğlu, Istanbul.
- **Phone**: +90 212 249 5930

Turkish Folk Music and Dance Performances

For a taste of traditional Turkish music and dance, head to the Istanbul Folklore Center or watch a Whirling Dervishes performance. These performances offer insight into Turkey's rich cultural traditions, from folk music to Sufi dances.

- **Address (Istanbul Folklore Center)**: Emin Ali Paşa Mahallesi, 34116 Fatih/Istanbul.
- **Phone**: +90 212 519 6778

Events And Festivals

Annual Festivals

Istanbul Film Festival

The Istanbul Film Festival, held every spring, is one of the city's most important cultural events. It showcases both Turkish and international films, and it's an excellent opportunity to see the latest films from up-and-coming filmmakers. The event includes screenings, special panels, and awards.

- **When**: April

Istanbul Music Festival

This festival is a highlight for music lovers. It brings together world-class classical musicians, orchestras, and soloists from

106

around the world to perform in Istanbul's historic venues, including the Istanbul Archaeological Museum and Hagia Irene.

- **When**: June

Istanbul Jazz Festival

Every summer, jazz enthusiasts flock to the Istanbul Jazz Festival. It features both local and international jazz musicians performing in various venues across the city. From intimate concerts in jazz clubs to large performances in open-air theaters, there's something for everyone.

- **When**: July

Istanbul Tulip Festival

A true celebration of spring, the Istanbul Tulip Festival brightens up the city each year. Public parks, gardens, and streets are covered in colorful tulips, creating a beautiful spectacle. You'll find the most vibrant displays in Emirgan Park and Gülhane Park.

- **When**: April

Major Events

Istanbul Marathon

The Istanbul Marathon is the only marathon in the world that connects two continents. Runners start in Asia and cross the Bosphorus Bridge to finish in Europe. It's an event not only for professional runners but also for amateur runners and walkers who want to experience the beauty of Istanbul while participating in a significant sporting event.

- **When**: November

Istanbul Biennial

The Istanbul Biennial is one of the most significant events for contemporary art. Every two years, this international art exhibition brings together artists from all over the world to showcase their works in museums, galleries, and public spaces throughout the city. The biennial is an opportunity to explore cutting-edge art and culture.

- **When**: Every two years, typically in September

Istanbul Fashion Week

This major fashion event is held in Istanbul and brings together top designers, models, and fashion enthusiasts. It's a chance to see the latest fashion trends and discover emerging Turkish designers.

- **When**: February or October (seasonal)

Cultural And Music Festivals

International Istanbul Theater Festival

For those who enjoy theater, the International Istanbul Theater Festival is a must-visit. The event features performances from local and international theater companies, including plays, experimental theater, and dance performances.

- **When**: May-June

Istanbul International Dance Festival

This event gathers dancers from around the world to perform in Istanbul. With a mix of workshops, performances, and social events, it's a great way to experience the art of dance.

- **When**: July

Rumi Festival

Celebrating the life of the famous poet and philosopher Rumi, this festival offers a rich blend of Sufi music, poetry readings, and spiritual gatherings. The festival usually takes place in the Mevlana Museum, where you can learn about the mystic's teachings and enjoy live performances.

- **When**: December

Food And Drink Festivals

Istanbul Food and Drink Festival

This event is a feast for food lovers. It brings together top chefs, restaurants, and food vendors who showcase a wide variety of Turkish and international dishes. There are cooking workshops, tastings, and food competitions to enjoy.

- **When**: October

Istanbul Coffee Festival

Coffee lovers will enjoy the Istanbul Coffee Festival, which celebrates the city's long-standing coffee culture. The festival offers coffee tastings, barista demonstrations, and talks about the history of Turkish coffee.

- **When**: September

Istanbul Wine Festival

Wine enthusiasts should not miss the Istanbul Wine Festival, which showcases wines from Turkish vineyards and international wine producers. Visitors can enjoy wine tastings, food pairings, and learn more about wine culture in Turkey.

- **When**: October

Istanbul Chocolate Festival

For those with a sweet tooth, the Istanbul Chocolate Festival is a must-attend. The festival features chocolates from around the world offering samples of their finest creations, along with workshops and demonstrations on how to make delicious chocolate treats.

- **When**: November

Day Trips And Excursions

Nearby Beach Resorts

1. Şile Beach

Located on the Black Sea coast, **Şile** is one of Istanbul's most popular beach destinations. It's a charming seaside town, known for its beautiful sandy beach and picturesque lighthouse. The calm and clean waters make it ideal for swimming, and the beach area has plenty of cafes and restaurants where you can enjoy local food and drinks. Apart from the beach, you can also explore nearby hiking trails and enjoy the natural scenery.

- **Address:** Şile, 34980 Istanbul, Turkey
- **Phone Number:** +90 216 721 4514 (local tourism office)

- **Travel Time from Istanbul:** Approximately 1.5 hours by car
- **Best Time to Visit:** June to September for the best weather

2. Kilyos Beach (Demirciköy)

If you're looking for a beach with a lively atmosphere and plenty of activities, **Kilyos** is a great choice. Located on the Black Sea coast, just 30 kilometers from Istanbul, Kilyos is known for its clean beaches, water sports opportunities (such as jet skiing and windsurfing), and vibrant beach clubs. The area also offers many outdoor restaurants and cafes where visitors can enjoy fresh seafood and local dishes.

- **Address:** Kilyos, Demirciköy, 34450 Sarıyer/Istanbul, Turkey

- **Phone Number:** +90 212 204 0177 (Kilyos Beach)
- **Travel Time from Istanbul:** 40–50 minutes by car
- **Best Time to Visit:** June to September

3. Prince Islands (Adalar)

The **Prince Islands**, located in the Sea of Marmara, offer a perfect escape from the hustle and bustle of Istanbul. These islands are accessible by ferry from Istanbul's Kabataş or Eminönü ports, and the trip takes around 1 to 1.5 hours. The largest island, **Büyükada**, is famous for its charming streets, historic buildings, and horse-drawn carriage rides. On the islands, you'll find quiet beaches where you can relax, swim, or enjoy water sports.

- **Address:** Büyükada, Heybeliada, Burgazada, Kınalıada (Adalar District), Istanbul, Turkey
- **Phone Number:** +90 216 382 9071 (Adalar Ferries)

- **Travel Time from Istanbul:** 1 to 1.5 hours by ferry from Kabataş or Eminönü
- **Best Time to Visit:** May to October

4. Şile Ağva Beach

A bit farther than the main beaches near Istanbul, **Ağva** is a peaceful village along the Black Sea, located around 1.5–2 hours away from the city. Known for its stunning beaches, clear waters, and serene environment, Ağva is perfect for a quiet beach day. Visitors can enjoy a boat ride along the **Goksu River**, explore nearby forests, or simply relax on the sandy shores.

- **Address:** Ağva, Şile, 34990 Istanbul, Turkey
- **Phone Number:** +90 216 721 4260 (Ağva Tourism Office)
- **Travel Time from Istanbul:** 1.5 to 2 hours by car
- **Best Time to Visit:** June to September

5. Florya Beach (Ataköy)

If you don't want to travel far, **Florya Beach**, located in the western part of Istanbul, is an excellent option for a quick getaway. The beach is located near the **Ataköy** neighborhood, offering a long stretch of sand along the Sea of Marmara. The area is very popular for families, and there are various facilities like cafes, restaurants, and public restrooms.

- **Address:** Florya, 34153 Bakırköy/Istanbul, Turkey
- **Phone Number:** +90 212 570 7602 (Florya Beach)
- **Travel Time from Istanbul:** Around 45 minutes by car
- **Best Time to Visit:** June to September

6. Caddebostan Beach (Asian Side)

For those staying in Istanbul's Asian side, **Caddebostan Beach** is a popular choice. Located on the coast of the Sea of Marmara, Caddebostan is a family-friendly area with several large parks, cafes, and a clean beach. The beach is easily accessible by public transportation, including buses and ferries. It's a great spot to spend a day relaxing by the sea or taking a stroll along the waterfront promenade.

- **Address:** Caddebostan, 34728 Kadıköy/Istanbul, Turkey
- **Phone Number:** +90 216 414 4422 (Caddebostan Beach)
- **Travel Time from Istanbul:** 25–30 minutes by car from Kadıköy
- **Best Time to Visit:** June to September

7. Poyrazköy Beach (Anadolu Hisarı)

For a more natural and less crowded beach experience, **Poyrazköy Beach** is a hidden gem on the Asian side of Istanbul. Located in the **Anadolu Hisarı** area, it's known for its natural beauty, clear waters, and quiet atmosphere. The beach is perfect for those who enjoy a peaceful day by the sea without the usual crowds.

- **Address:** Poyrazköy, 34810 Beykoz/Istanbul, Turkey
- **Phone Number:** +90 216 425 0507 (Poyrazköy Tourism Office)
- **Travel Time from Istanbul:** Around 1 hour by car
- **Best Time to Visit:** June to September

8. Ağva Gökçe Beach

Located in **Ağva**, **Gökçe Beach** offers visitors a quieter and more relaxed atmosphere compared to other beaches. With its shallow waters and natural surroundings, it's an excellent spot for families with children or anyone looking for a peaceful day by the sea. The area is surrounded by lush greenery and offers a perfect mix of the river and sea experience.

- **Address:** Gökçe Beach, Ağva, Şile, 34990 Istanbul, Turkey
- **Phone Number:** +90 216 721 4412 (local tourism office)
- **Travel Time from Istanbul:** Approximately 1.5 hours by car
- **Best Time to Visit:** June to September

Itineraries For Different Travelers

Weekend Getaway

Day 1: Historic Istanbul

- **Morning:** Start your day by visiting the **Hagia Sophia** (Sultanahmet Meydanı, 34122 Fatih, Istanbul, Turkey, +90 212 522 1750). This former church-turned-mosque-turned-museum is one of Istanbul's most iconic landmarks, with stunning Byzantine mosaics and Ottoman architecture.
- **Midday:** After Hagia Sophia, walk over to the **Blue Mosque** (Sultanahmet Square, 34122 Istanbul, Turkey,

+90 212 458 2240). It's free to enter, and its six minarets and magnificent interior make it a must-see.

- **Afternoon:** Visit the **Topkapi Palace** (Cankurtaran Mahallesi, 34122 Fatih, Istanbul, Turkey, +90 212 512 0480), the former residence of Ottoman sultans. Explore the stunning courtyards, gardens, and the palace's rich collection of imperial treasures.

- **Evening:** End your day with a stroll along **Istiklal Street** (Beyoğlu, Istanbul, Turkey). It's a lively pedestrian street lined with shops, cafes, and restaurants. Stop by **Taksim Square** (Taksim, Beyoğlu, 34437 Istanbul, Turkey) and enjoy dinner at one of the many local restaurants.

Day 2: Modern Istanbul & Bosphorus Cruise

- **Morning:** Start with a visit to the **Dolmabahçe Palace** (Vişnezade Mahallesi, Dolmabahçe Cd. No: 1, Beşiktaş, 34357 Istanbul, Turkey, +90 212 236 9000), a beautiful 19th-century palace on the Bosphorus. This site combines Ottoman and European architectural styles.

- **Afternoon:** Head to **Galata Tower** (Bereketzade, Galata Kulesi, 34421 Beyoğlu, Istanbul, Turkey, +90 212 293 8188). Climb to the top for panoramic views of Istanbul, including the Golden Horn and the Bosphorus.

- **Evening:** Relax with a **Bosphorus cruise**. Many tour companies offer short boat rides, usually lasting about an hour, providing a fantastic view of Istanbul from the water. A great starting point for the cruise is from **Eminönü Pier** (Eminönü, Istanbul, Turkey).

- **Dinner:** Have dinner in the **Karaköy** area, where you'll find modern eateries serving fresh seafood and local specialties.

Day 3: Relax and Explore Local Markets

- **Morning:** Head to the **Grand Bazaar** (Beyazıt, 34126 Fatih, Istanbul, Turkey, +90 212 519 1248). Wander through its hundreds of shops selling everything from jewelry to carpets, spices, and sweets.
- **Afternoon:** Explore the **Spice Bazaar** (Rüstem Paşa Mahallesi, 34116 Fatih, Istanbul, Turkey, +90 212 511 5180), another famous market, known for its exotic spices, Turkish delights, and teas.
- **Evening:** End your weekend with a relaxing dinner at a rooftop restaurant with views of the Bosphorus, such as **360 Istanbul** (İstiklal Caddesi, Beyoğlu, 34430 Istanbul, Turkey, +90 212 251 1042), offering modern Turkish cuisine and stunning city views.

Cultural Immersion

Day 1: Historical and Cultural Landmarks

- **Morning:** Visit **Hagia Sophia** and the **Blue Mosque** in Sultanahmet, as mentioned above. These historical sites

121

provide insight into the city's religious and architectural evolution.

- **Midday:** Head to the **Museum of Turkish and Islamic Arts** (Sultanahmet Square, 34122 Istanbul, Turkey, +90 212 518 1805), where you can view an extensive collection of Islamic calligraphy, textiles, and artifacts.
- **Afternoon:** Visit the **Basilica Cistern** (Alemdar Mahallesi, Yerebatan Caddesi No: 13, Sultanahmet, 34110 Istanbul, Turkey, +90 212 522 1259). This underground water reservoir built by Emperor Justinian in the 6th century is an impressive feat of engineering and history.

- **Evening:** Visit **Kadıköy** on the Asian side of Istanbul. Take the **ferry from Eminönü** (Eminönü, Istanbul,

Turkey) to Kadıköy, and wander around the lively **Kadıköy Market** (Kadıköy, Istanbul, Turkey). You'll find plenty of street food, live music, and art galleries here.

Day 2: Arts, Crafts, and Local Life

- **Morning:** Explore **Süleymaniye Mosque** (Süleymaniye Mahallesi, 34116 Fatih, Istanbul, Turkey, +90 212 458 0833), one of Istanbul's largest and most beautiful mosques, designed by the famous architect Mimar Sinan.
- **Midday:** Visit **Istanbul Modern Art Museum** (Kılıçali Paşa Mahallesi, Meclisi Mebusan Caddesi No: 4, Beyoğlu, 34433 Istanbul, Turkey, +90 212 334 7300). This museum showcases contemporary Turkish and international art.
- **Afternoon:** Stop by **Çukurcuma** (Çukurcuma, Beyoğlu, Istanbul, Turkey), a neighborhood known for its antique shops and galleries. You can explore the unique Turkish antiques and artworks on display.
- **Evening:** Experience Turkish culture through food by visiting a **Meze restaurant**. **Asmalı Cavit** (Asmalı Mescit Mahallesi, Asmalı Mescit Caddesi No: 16, Beyoğlu, 34430 Istanbul, Turkey, +90 212 292 5940) is known for serving traditional meze (small dishes) with raki, a Turkish aniseed drink.

Day 3: Local Communities & Crafts

- **Morning:** Visit **Emin Ali Paşa Mosque** (Emin Ali Paşa, 34134 Fatih, Istanbul, Turkey), a small yet historically rich mosque tucked away in a quiet corner of the city.
- **Midday:** Explore the **Fener & Balat districts**. These neighborhoods are known for their well-preserved Byzantine and Ottoman-era architecture. Visit the **Greek Patriarchal Cathedral of Fener** (Fener, Istanbul, Turkey), one of the oldest churches in Istanbul.
- **Afternoon:** Learn more about Turkish craftsmanship by visiting the **Turkish Carpets & Textile Museum** (İskenderpaşa Mahallesi, 34130 Fatih, Istanbul, Turkey, +90 212 639 6757). Here you can learn about the art of weaving and see the intricate patterns in carpets from different regions of Turkey.
- **Evening:** Head to the **Galata Bridge** (Galata Köprüsü, 34421 Beyoğlu, Istanbul, Turkey) to experience the local way of life. The bridge is often lined with fishermen, and it's a great spot to enjoy the sunset over the Bosphorus.

Outdoor Adventure

Day 1: Nature Walks & Bosphorus Views

- **Morning:** Begin your day with a hike in **Belgrad Forest** (Belgrad Ormanı, Bahçeköy, 34473 Istanbul, Turkey). This large forest park on the city's outskirts offers walking and cycling paths surrounded by lush greenery.

- **Midday:** After your hike, take a boat tour along the **Bosphorus**. Departing from **Kabataş Pier** (Kabataş, Beşiktaş, 34435 Istanbul, Turkey), you can enjoy stunning views of Istanbul from the water.
- **Afternoon:** Spend your afternoon at **Çamlıca Hill** (Çamlıca Tepesi, 34664 Üsküdar, Istanbul, Turkey). This hill offers panoramic views of Istanbul and is a great spot for a relaxing picnic or just enjoying the landscape.
- **Evening:** In the evening, head to **Kadıköy** (Kadıköy, Istanbul, Turkey) on the Asian side, where you can relax at one of the waterfront cafes and enjoy the sunset over the Sea of Marmara.

Day 2: Urban Hiking & Parks

- **Morning:** Start with a walk through **Gülhane Park** (Gülhane Parkı, Sultanahmet, 34122 Istanbul, Turkey), a historical park located near Topkapi Palace. It's a peaceful place with beautiful greenery, perfect for a morning stroll or a light jog. The park also has benches where you can rest and enjoy the view of the Bosphorus.
- **Midday:** After exploring Gülhane Park, head to **Yıldız Park** (Yıldız Mh., 34349 Beşiktaş, Istanbul, Turkey), a large and serene park located between Beşiktaş and Ortaköy. It's perfect for nature lovers and offers a mix of walking paths, ponds, and shaded areas. You can even explore the Yıldız Palace located within the park.

- **Afternoon:** Visit **Ortaköy Square** (Ortaköy Mahallesi, 34347 Beşiktaş, Istanbul, Turkey), where you can enjoy the stunning views of the **Bosphorus Bridge**. The square is filled with street vendors selling Turkish snacks, such as kumpir (stuffed baked potatoes) and simit (sesame-crusted bread rings).

- **Evening:** For an active evening, take a walk or rent a bike along **Beyoğlu's Istiklal Street** (Beyoğlu, Istanbul, Turkey), which is closed to traffic. This pedestrian street is lively and stretches for over a mile, offering a fun experience for both locals and tourists. There are plenty of cafes, restaurants, and shops to stop by as you explore.

Day 3: Adventure on the Islands

- **Morning:** Take a ferry ride to the **Princes' Islands**, a group of nine islands in the Sea of Marmara. The most popular island for outdoor activities is **Büyükada** (Büyükada, 34970 Istanbul, Turkey), where you can rent a bike or enjoy a peaceful walk. The island is car-free, which makes it perfect for cycling or horse-drawn carriage rides through the picturesque streets.
- **Midday:** Explore the **Aya Yorgi Church** (Büyükada, 34970, Istanbul, Turkey), located at the top of a hill. The climb is a bit steep, but once you reach the top, you'll be rewarded with spectacular views of the island and the surrounding sea.
- **Afternoon:** After your hike or bike ride, relax at one of the beach clubs on the island, such as **Nena Beach Club** (Büyükada, 34970, Istanbul, Turkey). Enjoy swimming in the clear waters or simply relax by the seaside with a refreshing drink.
- **Evening:** Head back to the mainland and finish your adventure with a visit to **Emirgan Park** (Emirgan Mahallesi, 34467 Beşiktaş, Istanbul, Turkey), one of Istanbul's largest and most famous parks. The park offers excellent spots for evening walks and has beautiful views of the Bosphorus, making it the perfect spot to unwind after your outdoor adventure.

Family-Friendly Trip

Day 1:

- **Morning:** Start your day at **Miniaturk** (Imrahor Caddesi, Sütlüce, 34445, Istanbul, Turkey). This park showcases miniatures of famous landmarks in Turkey, making it an entertaining and educational stop for families. Children can enjoy seeing replicas of historical buildings and monuments in a large open space. Entry fee: 15 TL. Phone: +90 212 222 3366.

- **Afternoon:** Head to **Istanbul Aquarium** (Florya Mahallesi, Yeşilköy, 34153, Istanbul, Turkey). This massive aquarium has over 1,500 species of marine life and also features a rainforest section and interactive exhibits. It's perfect for kids to explore the underwater world and have fun learning about marine creatures. Entry fee: 40 TL. Phone: +90 212 444 6655.

- **Evening:** Visit **Gülhane Park** (Gülhane Parkı, Sultanahmet, 34112, Istanbul, Turkey), located next to Topkapi Palace. The park is spacious, with plenty of green areas for kids to run and play. You can enjoy a picnic while the children explore the playgrounds. It's a peaceful spot for winding down after a day of adventure.

Day 2:

- **Morning:** Spend the morning at **Vialand Theme Park** (Peyami Safa Cd. 21, Eyüp, Istanbul, Turkey). This amusement park offers thrilling rides, a shopping mall, and entertainment shows that are great for kids and teens. From roller coasters to smaller rides for younger children, there's something for everyone. Entry fee: 50 TL for the theme park. Phone: +90 212 495 55 55.

- **Afternoon:** After lunch, visit **Istanbul Toy Museum** (Osmanağa Mahallesi, 34714 Kadıköy, Istanbul, Turkey). The museum showcases a collection of toys from different countries and historical periods. It's a fun and nostalgic stop for children to learn about the history of toys while playing with some of the displays. Entry fee: 15 TL. Phone: +90 216 359 6034.

- **Evening:** End the day with a visit to **Emirgan Park** (Emirgan Mahallesi, 34467 Beşiktaş, Istanbul, Turkey). This large park has playgrounds, walking paths, and scenic views of the Bosphorus. It's a great place for the whole family to enjoy a leisurely stroll and relax. There are also cafes for a family-friendly meal.

Budget Travel

Day 1:

- **Morning:** Start with a visit to the iconic **Sultanahmet Square** (Sultanahmet, 34122 Istanbul, Turkey), home to famous landmarks like the **Blue Mosque** and **Hagia Sophia**. These historical sites are free to visit, and you can admire the architecture and history without spending a dime. The Blue Mosque is open every day except during prayer times, and Hagia Sophia is free to enter.

- **Afternoon:** Head to **Basilica Cistern** (Yerebatan Caddesi, Sultanahmet, 34110 Istanbul, Turkey), an ancient underground water storage facility. The entrance fee is around 20 TL. It's a cool, peaceful place to escape the crowds and explore Istanbul's history. Phone: +90 212 522 1259.
- **Evening:** For dinner, try local Turkish street food. **Simit Sarayı** (Various locations throughout Istanbul) offers delicious and inexpensive simit (Turkish sesame bagels) and other snacks. You can also grab a quick meal of döner kebab or börek (savory pastries) from street vendors around Sultanahmet.

Day 2:

- **Morning:** Take a free walk around **Taksim Square** (Taksim, Beyoğlu, Istanbul, Turkey), a lively area filled with shops, cafes, and restaurants. Walk down **Istiklal Street** (Beyoğlu, Istanbul, Turkey), where you can window shop, grab affordable snacks, and take in the atmosphere. There are free events and performances in the square at times.
- **Afternoon:** Visit **Çukurcuma Antique Street** (Çukurcuma Caddesi, Beyoğlu, Istanbul, Turkey). This area is lined with quirky antique shops and second-hand stores. It's a great place to explore without spending money, or if you want to pick up an affordable souvenir.

- **Evening:** For dinner, head to **Kadıköy Market** (Kadıköy, Istanbul, Turkey). Here, you'll find inexpensive fresh food markets, restaurants, and cafes. You can enjoy a budget-friendly dinner of fresh fish, olives, or Turkish meze (small dishes).

Solo Traveler's Guide

Day 1:

- **Morning:** Start with a peaceful visit to the **Hagia Sophia** (Sultanahmet, 34122 Istanbul, Turkey), one of Istanbul's most famous landmarks. It's a great place to reflect, take photos, and enjoy the architecture. The entrance fee is 100 TL, and it's open daily from 9 AM to 7 PM.

- **Afternoon:** Explore **Karaköy** (Karaköy, Beyoğlu, Istanbul, Turkey), a trendy neighborhood that's perfect for solo wanderers. You can stroll around, enjoy the street art, visit local shops, and relax in cafes. Stop for a coffee at **Karaköy Güllüoğlu** (Karaköy, 34425 Istanbul, Turkey), a popular spot for Turkish pastries.
- **Evening:** For a unique experience, go for a **Bosphorus Cruise** (Kabataş, Istanbul, Turkey), where you can enjoy beautiful views of the city. The cruise offers a peaceful way to see Istanbul from the water, especially during sunset. The boat ride costs around 25 TL for a short tour.

Day 2:

- **Morning:** Visit the **Istanbul Modern Art Museum** (Meclisi Mebusan Caddesi, Beyoğlu, 34433, Istanbul, Turkey). It's a perfect spot for solo travelers who love art and culture. The museum displays contemporary art from Turkish and international artists. Entry fee: 40 TL. Phone: +90 212 334 7300.
- **Afternoon:** Explore the streets of **Fener and Balat** (Fener, Istanbul, Turkey), two historic neighborhoods with colorful houses and hidden gems. It's a great place for solo travelers to wander without a set itinerary. Visit the **Greek Orthodox Patriarchal Cathedral** (Fener, Istanbul, Turkey) and discover unique local spots.

- **Evening:** End your day at **Galata Tower** (Bereketzade, 34421 Beyoğlu, Istanbul, Turkey). For a small fee (35 TL), you can take an elevator up to the top for panoramic views of the city. It's a great way to reflect on your journey and enjoy a view of Istanbul's skyline.

Romantic Getaways

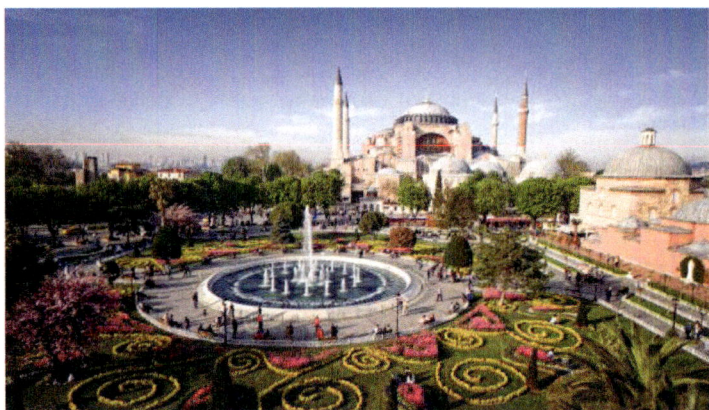

Day 1:

- **Morning:** Begin with a visit to **Topkapi Palace** (Cankurtaran, Sultanahmet, 34122 Istanbul, Turkey). Explore the palace's beautiful gardens, courtyards, and the Harem section. It's a peaceful, historical spot to start your romantic journey. The entry fee is around 40 TL. Phone: +90 212 512 0480.
- **Afternoon:** Take a **Bosphorus Cruise** (Kabataş, Istanbul, Turkey) together to enjoy the stunning views of

the Bosphorus Strait. The cruise is a fantastic way to see the city from the water, with picturesque sights of bridges, palaces, and the old city.

- **Evening:** Enjoy a romantic dinner at **Mikla Restaurant** (The Marmara Pera Hotel, Meşrutiyet Cd. No:15, 34430 Beyoğlu, Istanbul, Turkey), a rooftop restaurant offering a stunning view of the city skyline. Reservations are recommended. Phone: +90 212 293 5656.

Day 2:

- **Morning:** Visit **Pierre Loti Café** (Eyüp, Istanbul, Turkey), located on top of a hill with incredible views of the Golden Horn. You can take the cable car up for a unique experience. The café is perfect for enjoying a cup of Turkish tea with your loved one while overlooking the city.

- **Afternoon:** Explore **Emirgan Park** (Emirgan Mahallesi, 34467 Beşiktaş, Istanbul, Turkey). The park offers spacious walking paths, beautiful gardens, and the opportunity to relax and enjoy nature together. It's a peaceful spot, ideal for a quiet afternoon.

- **Evening:** End your romantic day with a sunset visit to **Galata Tower** (Bereketzade, 34421 Beyoğlu, Istanbul, Turkey). As you ascend the tower, you and your partner can enjoy breathtaking panoramic views of the city as the sun sets over the Bosphorus. It's the perfect romantic setting to share a quiet moment together. The entry fee is 35 TL. Phone: +90 212 293 8130.

- Afterwards, take a romantic stroll through **Istiklal Street** (Beyoğlu, Istanbul, Turkey). This iconic street is lined with beautiful historical buildings, cafés, and boutiques. It's a lovely place to wander, stop for a coffee, and watch the vibrant nightlife unfold.

Health And Safety

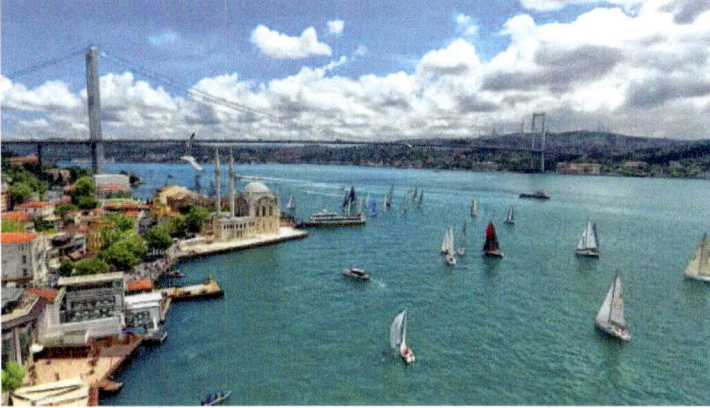

Health Precautions

- **Drinking Water**: It's safe to drink tap water in most places in Istanbul, but if you're uncertain about the water quality, it's always better to stick to bottled water. You can buy bottled water from almost any convenience store or supermarket.

- **Vaccinations**: Before traveling to Istanbul, ensure you are up-to-date on routine vaccinations such as Hepatitis A, Hepatitis B, and Typhoid, especially if you plan on visiting local markets or rural areas. The **Centers for Disease Control and Prevention (CDC)** recommends certain vaccines for travelers to Turkey, so it's best to consult with a healthcare provider.

- **Air Pollution**: Istanbul experiences air pollution during certain times of the year. If you're sensitive to air quality, consider wearing a mask and limiting outdoor activities on days with poor air quality.
- **Mosquitoes**: In the summer months, mosquitoes are more active, especially near parks or water. It's advisable to use insect repellent and wear long sleeves and pants in the evenings.
- **Health Insurance**: Make sure you have travel insurance that covers health emergencies, as medical care can be expensive without it. Many travel insurance plans offer coverage for hospital visits, medications, and medical evacuation.

Safety Tips

- **Be Mindful of Your Belongings**: As in any large city, pickpocketing can happen in busy areas such as **Taksim Square** or on public transportation. Always keep your wallet, phone, and other valuables secure and avoid carrying large amounts of cash.
- **Use Reputable Transportation**: When using taxis, ensure you take licensed ones. You can recognize licensed taxis by the yellow color and the "Taksi" sign. Always agree on the fare before starting the ride or ensure the meter is running. If you're using ride-sharing services like

Uber or **BiTaksi**, make sure your ride matches the details on the app.

- **Avoid Isolated Areas After Dark**: While Istanbul is generally safe, it's a good idea to avoid quiet and poorly lit streets late at night, especially in unfamiliar neighborhoods. Stick to well-lit areas with other people around.

- **Stay Alert in Tourist Spots**: Tourist-heavy spots like **Sultanahmet**, **Grand Bazaar**, and **Istiklal Street** can be crowded, and distractions may be used to steal from unsuspecting travelers. Be cautious of overly friendly strangers who approach you out of nowhere.

Common Scams And How To Avoid Them

- **The "Fake Tour Guides" Scam**: Some individuals may approach you claiming to be tour guides and offer you a "free" tour of major sights. While most are just trying to make money by selling expensive tours or services, some can be aggressive in their tactics. To avoid this scam, always book tours through reputable agencies or official tourist information centers.

- **Fake Currency**: Although rare, counterfeit bills can sometimes circulate. Always check your change before leaving a store or restaurant, especially in high-volume tourist areas. Using credit cards or withdrawing cash from ATMs inside banks can help minimize the risk.

- **The "Spilled Drink" Scam**: A scam artist may "accidentally" spill something on you while you're sitting in a café or restaurant, then offer to clean it up and help you. During this, their accomplice might steal your bag or belongings. If this happens, stay alert and keep your bag in sight.
- **Overcharging in Tourist Areas**: Some restaurants or shops in touristy areas like **Sultanahmet** might overcharge tourists, so it's a good idea to check the menu prices before sitting down or buying. It's also wise to ask for the bill to be shown to you before paying.
- **Street Performers**: You might encounter street performers in popular spots asking for tips. While this is common, some might be more aggressive than others. It's up to you whether to give a tip, but if you don't want to, be polite but firm when declining.

Emergency Contacts And Services

- **Emergency Services (Police, Ambulance, Fire)**: 112 (This number works for both police and ambulance services, and they can help with any urgent situation).
- **Tourist Police**: 0212 527 4507. The tourist police in Istanbul can assist with any issues involving tourists, including lost passports or reporting a crime.

- **Lost Property**: If you lose your belongings, contact the nearest police station. You can also check with **Istanbul Lost and Found** (Phone: 0212 555 1060) to see if they have recovered your lost items.

- **Hospitals**: There are many hospitals in Istanbul where you can get medical assistance if needed. Some of the well-known ones include:

  - **American Hospital** (Abide-i Hürriyet Cd. No: 340, 34381 Şişli, Istanbul, Turkey). Phone: +90 212 311 2000. This hospital provides excellent healthcare for international travelers.

  - **Florence Nightingale Hospital** (Büyükdere Cd. No: 149, 34394 Şişli, Istanbul, Turkey). Phone: +90 212 320 2111.

- **Pharmacies**: If you need a pharmacy, most areas in Istanbul have 24-hour pharmacies (Eczane). A well-known one in **Taksim** is the **Taksim Pharmacy** located at **Sıraselviler Cd. No: 27, 34430 Beyoğlu, Istanbul**. Phone: +90 212 293 3954.

Money And Budgeting In Istanbul

Currency Exchange

The local currency in Istanbul is the **Turkish Lira (TRY)**. Most businesses in Istanbul accept the Turkish Lira, but some may also accept foreign currencies like **Euros** or **US Dollars**, especially in tourist areas. However, it's always a good idea to have Turkish Lira for everyday expenses to avoid extra charges when converting your money.

Where to Exchange Money:

- **Currency Exchange Offices (Döviz)**: These are the most common places to exchange foreign currency into

Turkish Lira. They are available at airports, shopping malls, and popular tourist areas like **Sultanahmet** and **Taksim Square**. However, always check the exchange rate offered before proceeding.

- **Banks**: Banks in Istanbul also offer currency exchange, and their rates are generally more favorable than those at exchange offices. Some of the well-known banks with exchange services include **Ziraat Bank** (located at various locations, including **Taksim**). You can visit a bank branch and exchange your foreign currency into Turkish Lira.

- **Airport Exchange**: While airports offer convenient exchange services, the rates are often less favorable compared to currency exchange offices or banks. Therefore, it's recommended to exchange only a small amount of money at the airport if necessary.

Exchange Rates: Keep in mind that exchange rates can fluctuate. It's a good idea to check current rates online or on your phone using a currency converter app to ensure you're getting a good deal. Some exchange offices might also charge a commission or offer slightly worse rates for small transactions.

Tipping And Gratuities

Restaurants: In restaurants, a tip of about **5% to 10%** of the total bill is considered polite. Some places may already include a service charge, so it's worth checking your bill to avoid tipping twice. If no service charge is included, you can leave a small cash tip directly to the waiter or waitress.

Taxis: It's common to round up the fare to the nearest **5 or 10 Lira**. If the taxi ride is very long or the driver is especially helpful, you can add a little more. For example, if the fare is 50 Lira, you can round it up to 55 Lira.

Hotel Staff:

- **Hotel Bellboys**: If someone helps you with your luggage, a tip of **5 to 10 Lira** is appropriate.
- **Housekeeping**: Leaving a tip of **5 to 10 Lira per night** for housekeeping staff is a kind gesture.
- **Concierge**: If you receive excellent service from the concierge, consider tipping around **20 Lira**, especially if they've arranged special services like bookings or tours.

Tour Guides: For guided tours, a tip of **10 to 20 Lira** per person for a full-day tour is a good guideline. If you're happy with the service, you can tip more.

Budgeting Tips

Accommodation: Accommodation in Istanbul ranges from budget-friendly hostels to five-star luxury hotels. Staying in tourist areas like **Sultanahmet** or **Taksim** might be more expensive, but it's also more convenient. If you want to save money, consider staying in neighborhoods like **Karaköy**, **Beşiktaş**, or **Kadıköy**, which offer affordable hotels and guesthouses with easy access to major attractions.

- Budget option: **Cheers Hostel** in Sultanahmet offers affordable dormitory-style rooms and private rooms.
- Mid-range: **The Marmara Taksim** is a nice option with moderate prices located in the heart of Taksim Square.

Food: You can eat well in Istanbul without breaking the bank. There are plenty of inexpensive options available, especially in local restaurants or street food stalls.

- **Street Food**: Try a **simit** (Turkish sesame bagel) or a **kebap** from one of the many street vendors for just a few lira. A **balık ekmek** (fish sandwich) near **Eminönü** is another affordable option.
- **Local Restaurants**: Enjoy a full meal at a mid-range restaurant for around **50 to 100 Lira** per person. You'll find great options in neighborhoods like **Kadıköy** or **Galata**.
- **Fine Dining**: For a more luxurious experience, expect to pay more, but Istanbul also offers many reasonably priced fine dining spots. For example, **Mikla** is known for its views and gourmet Turkish dishes (price per person can range from 200 to 400 Lira).

Public Transportation: Istanbul has an affordable and efficient public transportation system that includes buses, trams, ferries, and the metro. You can buy an **Istanbulkart** (travel card) for easy access to all modes of transportation. The card can be purchased at vending machines or kiosks in metro stations and costs **10 Lira** for the card plus a top-up for fares. Each trip will cost between **3 to 7 Lira**, depending on the mode of transportation and distance.

Attractions: Many of Istanbul's attractions are free or have low entrance fees.

- **Topkapi Palace**: Entrance is around **100 Lira** (you can also pay extra for the harem).
- **Basilica Cistern**: Entry fee is **20 Lira**.
- **Blue Mosque**: Free to enter, but donations are encouraged.
- **Grand Bazaar and Spice Bazaar**: Free to visit; just be mindful of how much you spend on souvenirs.

Finding Deals And Discounts

- **Tourist Passes**: Consider buying an Istanbul Tourist Pass, which provides access to many of the city's top attractions, including the **Topkapi Palace**, **Hagia Sophia**, and **Basilica Cistern**, all for a fixed price. The pass can save you money if you plan to visit several popular sites.

- **Discounted Tickets**: Look out for special offers and discounts at attractions. Some museums and historic sites offer discounts during off-peak times or for students and seniors.
- **Free Events**: Istanbul has plenty of free events throughout the year, including art exhibitions, concerts, and festivals. Check local listings or visit **Istanbul's official tourism website** for updates on free activities during your stay.
- **Off-Season Travel**: Traveling during the off-season (usually between November and March) can save you money on flights, accommodation, and attractions. The weather is cooler, and there are fewer crowds.
- **Bargaining in Markets**: When shopping in markets like the **Grand Bazaar** or **Spice Bazaar**, don't be afraid to haggle. Prices are often negotiable, and you can usually get a better deal if you're willing to negotiate with the vendor.

Local Customs And Etiquette

Social Norms

- **Respect for Elders**: Turkish society places a high value on respect for older people. It's common to stand when an elder enters a room, and you may see younger people offering their seat to older passengers on public transportation. When interacting with older people, use polite forms of address, such as "Bey" (for Mr.) or "Hanım" (for Mrs.).

- **Personal Space**: While Istanbul is a large, busy city, people tend to value personal space in certain situations. However, during busy times in public places, especially in markets and crowded streets, you may find that personal space is limited. Just be patient and polite if you find yourself in close quarters with others.

- **Hospitality**: Turkish people are known for their hospitality. It's common for locals to invite strangers for a drink or tea, especially in more traditional areas. If you are invited to someone's home, it is customary to bring a small gift, such as sweets or flowers, as a sign of appreciation.
- **Gender Norms**: Turkey is a relatively conservative country, and although Istanbul is quite progressive compared to other regions of Turkey, it's still important to be aware of gender norms. Women and men are generally treated equally in many areas, especially in the city, but it's best to avoid overly intimate behavior, like public displays of affection, in more traditional settings.

Dining Etiquette

- **Mealtimes**: The main meal of the day is usually served in the evening, between 7 PM and 9 PM. Breakfast (kahvaltı) is typically lighter, with items like bread, cheese, olives, tomatoes, and eggs. Lunch is often a quick and lighter meal, but dinner is usually more substantial.
- **Sharing Food**: Turkish meals are often served family-style, meaning that several dishes are placed in the center of the table, and everyone shares. It's considered

impolite to take more than your share or to leave a plate completely empty if there is food left over.

- **Saying "Afiyet Olsun"**: When someone offers you food, it's polite to say "Afiyet olsun," which means "enjoy your meal." If you're the one serving, saying this to others shows good manners.

- **Tea and Coffee**: Turkish people love tea and coffee. Offering tea is a common gesture of hospitality, especially in shops or markets. Don't be surprised if you're offered a cup of **çay** (Turkish tea) when shopping or meeting with locals. Similarly, Turkish coffee is an important part of the culture and is typically served in small cups after a meal.

- **Eating with Hands**: While most meals are eaten with utensils, it's not uncommon to use your hands for certain foods, like **lahmacun** (Turkish pizza) or **köfte** (meatballs). If you use your hands, always do so with your right hand, as the left hand is considered less clean.

Dress Code

- **Modesty**: While Istanbul is a modern city, it's a good idea to dress modestly, particularly when visiting religious sites such as **mosques**. Women should have their heads covered (a scarf is fine), and both men and women should avoid wearing shorts or sleeveless tops when visiting these places. In other parts of the city, you'll see people wearing a wide range of clothing, from casual wear to more formal attire.

- **Casual Wear**: Istanbul is home to a vibrant fashion scene, and you'll see a variety of styles, from modern clothing to traditional outfits. It's common to wear casual, comfortable clothes, especially when sightseeing. However, if you plan to visit upscale restaurants, bars, or theaters, it's a good idea to wear more formal attire (smart casual or dressy).

- **Footwear**: When walking around the city, comfortable shoes are important because the streets can be cobbled or uneven, especially in older areas like **Sultanahmet**. Sneakers, flats, or walking shoes are ideal. If you plan to visit religious sites, you may be asked to remove your shoes, so wear socks or comfortable sandals.

- **Religious Sites**: As mentioned earlier, when visiting mosques, women should wear a scarf to cover their hair and avoid wearing revealing clothes. Men should also avoid wearing shorts and should cover their arms. Both men and women must remove their shoes before entering a mosque.

Greetings And Interactions

- **Handshakes**: A handshake is a common greeting in Istanbul, especially for people who have just met. It's generally polite to offer a firm but not overly strong handshake, and it's respectful to greet others by using their title (e.g., Mr., Mrs.) followed by their last name.

- **Kissing on the Cheek**: Among friends and family, it's common to greet each other with a kiss on both cheeks. However, this is typically reserved for people you know well, and not for strangers or casual acquaintances.

- **Using "Merhaba"**: The most common greeting in Turkish is **"Merhaba"**, which means "Hello." It's used in almost any situation, from meeting someone for the first time to greeting a friend. You can also use **"Günaydın"** (Good morning) and **"İyi akşamlar"** (Good evening) depending on the time of day.

- **Respectful Interactions**: In Istanbul, as in the rest of Turkey, it's important to be polite in your interactions. Always say **"Lütfen"** (please) and **"Teşekkür ederim"** (thank you) when making requests or accepting something. People appreciate these basic gestures of kindness and respect.

- **Respect for Personal Boundaries**: While Turkish people are generally friendly and open, it's important to respect personal boundaries, especially when interacting with strangers. Avoid asking overly personal questions unless you have established a good rapport with someone.

Language And Useful Phrases In Istanbul

Basic Turkish Phrases

Here are some basic phrases that can help you navigate everyday situations in Istanbul:

- **Merhaba** – Hello

   This is the most common greeting in Turkish. You can use it any time of the day when meeting someone.
- **Günaydın** – Good morning

   Use this greeting when you meet someone early in the day, before noon.

- **İyi akşamlar** – Good evening

  Use this phrase in the evening when greeting someone.
- **İyi geceler** – Good night

  This is used when you're saying goodbye for the night or wishing someone a peaceful sleep.
- **Hoşça kal** – Goodbye (when you are leaving)

  This is a casual way to say goodbye. If someone else is leaving, you can say **"Güle güle"**, which means "Go with a smile."
- **Lütfen** – Please

  A polite way to ask for something or make a request.
- **Teşekkür ederim** – Thank you

  When you want to express your thanks, use this phrase. If you want to be even more polite, you can say **"Çok teşekkür ederim,"** meaning "Thank you very much."
- **Evet** – Yes

  This is the Turkish word for "yes."
- **Hayır** – No

  Use this word to say "no."
- **Afedersiniz** – Excuse me / I'm sorry

  This is a polite way to get someone's attention or apologize.
- **Bilmiyorum** – I don't know

  A simple way to express that you don't know something.
- **Nasılsınız?** – How are you?

  This is a polite and formal way to ask someone how they

are. If you're talking to a friend or someone younger, you can say **"Nasılsın?"**

- **İyi** – Good

  If someone asks how you are, you can reply with **"İyi,"** meaning "good."

- **Ne kadar?** – How much?

  This is a useful phrase when shopping or asking the price of something.

- **Tuvalet nerede?** – Where is the bathroom?

  This is a very important phrase to know when you need to find a restroom.

- **Yardım eder misiniz?** – Can you help me?

  A polite way to ask for assistance.

- **Evet, biraz Türkçe konuşabiliyorum.** – Yes, I can speak a little Turkish.

  If you want to let someone know that you can speak a little Turkish, this phrase will help.

Common Expressions

Here are some expressions you'll hear frequently in Istanbul that will help you understand the local language better:

- **Nasılsın?** – How are you?

  This is a casual way to ask someone how they are, usually used among friends or people you know well.

- **Benim adım...** – My name is...

  Use this phrase when introducing yourself to someone.

- **Ne yapıyorsun?** – What are you doing?

  A common question when talking to friends or people you are familiar with.

- **Teşekkürler** – Thanks

  This is a more casual or shorter version of **"Teşekkür ederim."** It's used among friends or in informal settings.

- **Affedersiniz, pardon** – Excuse me, sorry

  Use this when you need to get someone's attention or if you've made a mistake.

- **Hoş geldiniz!** – Welcome!

  This is a warm greeting you can expect to hear when you arrive in a store, restaurant, or even at someone's home.

- **Bunu seviyorum** – I like this

  This is a helpful phrase if you want to express that you like something.

- **Lütfen biraz daha yavaş konuşur musunuz?** – Could you speak a little slower, please?

  This phrase is helpful if you're struggling to understand someone speaking quickly in Turkish.

- **Yavaş, lütfen** – Slowly, please

  If you want to ask someone to slow down when speaking, this is a simple way to request it.

- **Anlamadım** – I don't understand

  Use this when you need help with something you're unable to understand.

- **Ne zaman?** – When?

  A helpful phrase when you need to know when something will happen.

- **Bu ne?** – What is this?

  This is a useful phrase when you're exploring or shopping and want to know what something is.

- **Süper!** – Great!

  You can use this to express excitement or approval. It's the Turkish equivalent of "super" or "awesome."

Essential Vocabulary

Knowing these words can be very helpful in everyday conversations and situations:

- **Evet / Hayır** – Yes / No

  Very important for making simple decisions and responses.

- **Burası çok güzel** – This is very beautiful

  Use this when you want to compliment a place you're visiting or a view you like.

- **Çok güzel** – Very nice / Beautiful

  This is a common expression of appreciation, whether for a person, place, or thing.

- **Herkes** – Everyone

  A good word to know if you're talking about a group of people.

- **Birkaç** – A few

  Use this to refer to a small number of things.
- **Büyük** – Big

  Useful for describing something large or important.
- **Küçük** – Small

  The opposite of **"büyük,"** which you'll use to describe something small.
- **Ekmek** – Bread

  Bread is a staple in Turkish cuisine, and this is the word for it.
- **Su** – Water

  If you're thirsty, this is the word to use when asking for water.
- **Yemek** – Food / Meal

  A very important word if you're talking about eating or food.
- **Saat** – Time / Clock

  If you want to ask the time or refer to a clock, you can use this word.
- **Market** – Store / Market

  This is the word you'll use when you need to buy food or other items.
- **Bira** – Beer

  If you're interested in trying a local drink, **"bira"** is the Turkish word for beer.

- **Şarap** – Wine

  The Turkish word for wine, which is common in the country's food and dining culture.

- **Hastane** – Hospital

  It's important to know this word in case of emergencies.

- **Polis** – Police

  The word you'll use if you need to contact the authorities.

- **Doktor** – Doctor

  If you need medical assistance, this is the word for doctor.

- **Zarf** – Envelope

  A useful word when you need to send a letter or handle mail.

What To Do And Not To Do

Do's

Do Dress Modestly When Visiting Religious Sites

- Turkey is a predominantly Muslim country, and it's important to show respect when visiting mosques or other religious sites. For men and women, it's recommended to wear modest clothing, covering your shoulders and legs. Women may need to cover their hair with a scarf, especially in mosques.

Do Use Polite Greetings

- Turkish people appreciate it when visitors make an effort to greet them in Turkish. Saying "Merhaba" (Hello) or "Teşekkür ederim" (Thank you) can go a long way in building a friendly rapport with locals.

Do Bargain in Markets

- Bargaining is a common practice in Turkish bazaars like the Grand Bazaar or Spice Bazaar. Vendors expect a bit of negotiation, so don't be shy to ask for a discount. However, always keep it friendly and respectful.

Do Respect Local Traditions and Customs

- Respect local customs, such as taking off your shoes when entering someone's home or a mosque. This shows respect for the space and the people you are visiting.

Do Try Turkish Food

- Turkish cuisine is a highlight of the country, and you should definitely try local dishes like kebabs, baklava, and pide. Street food is also a fun experience, with vendors selling simit (a type of bread), chestnuts, and fish sandwiches along the Bosphorus.

Do Use Public Transport

- Istanbul has an efficient public transportation system, including trams, buses, and ferries. It's a great way to explore the city at a low cost, and it's often the fastest way to get around. Make sure to buy an Istanbulkart, a transport card that gives you easy access to most public transport options.

Do Keep Small Change for Tips

- Tipping is common in Istanbul and appreciated by restaurant staff, hotel staff, and taxi drivers. While tipping is not mandatory, it's good to leave a small tip for good service.

Do Be Patient

- Turkish people are known for their hospitality, and they are often willing to go out of their way to help tourists. If you need assistance, be patient, as the pace of life in Istanbul can be slower compared to Western countries.

Do Visit Istanbul's Famous Landmarks

- Be sure to visit the city's iconic sites such as the Hagia Sophia, the Blue Mosque, the Bosphorus Bridge, and Topkapi Palace. These landmarks offer a glimpse into Istanbul's rich history and culture.

Don'ts

Don't Take Photos in Restricted Areas

- While Istanbul is full of beautiful photo opportunities, always ask for permission before taking photos, especially in religious places or private spaces. Some mosques or museums may have restrictions on photography.

Don't Publicly Display Affection

- Public displays of affection, such as kissing or hugging, are not widely accepted in public spaces, especially in more conservative areas of Istanbul. It's best to keep such acts private or in more liberal areas like cafes or parks.

Don't Expect People to Speak English Everywhere

- While many people in Istanbul, particularly in tourist areas, understand some English, don't expect everyone to speak it fluently. Learning a few basic Turkish phrases will be appreciated, but always be prepared for language barriers, especially in less touristy areas.

Don't Point Your Feet at People

- In Turkish culture, pointing your feet at people, especially when sitting, is considered rude. If you're sitting cross-legged, be mindful of where your feet are pointing.

Don't Engage in Heated Arguments

- Turkish people are known for their hospitality and respect for guests, so it's important to maintain a respectful tone in conversations, especially with locals. Avoid engaging in arguments, particularly about politics or religion, as these topics can be sensitive.

Don't Enter Mosques During Prayer Time (If Not Participating)

- If you're visiting a mosque during prayer time, it's best to wait outside or visit after the prayers are finished. If you're not Muslim, it's respectful to avoid entering the mosque while prayers are taking place, as the space is reserved for worshippers.

Don't Disrespect Local Customs

- Avoid making negative comments about Turkey's culture or religion. This is considered disrespectful and can cause tension. Show respect for the country and its people by embracing the local customs and traditions.

Don't Expect Bargains Everywhere

- While bargaining is common in markets like the Grand Bazaar, it's not appropriate everywhere. In regular stores or restaurants, the prices are fixed, and trying to negotiate can be seen as rude.

Don't Overdo Alcohol Consumption

- While drinking alcohol is legal and quite common in Istanbul, overindulgence is not culturally accepted, especially in public places or religious areas. Drink responsibly and be mindful of the setting.

Cultural Sensitivities

Respect for Elders

- In Turkish culture, elders are highly respected. It's important to show deference to older individuals. For instance, if you are on public transport, it is customary to offer your seat to elderly people, especially women.

Respect for Religion

- Religion plays a significant role in Turkish society. Islam is the dominant religion, and you'll see many people following religious practices, such as prayer and fasting during Ramadan. Being respectful of these practices, even if you're not Muslim, is important. For example, try to avoid eating or drinking in public during the daytime in Ramadan.

Offer Help to Locals in Need

- Turkish people have a strong sense of community. If you see someone struggling or in need, it's common to offer help, especially if they're elderly or carrying something heavy.

Gift Giving Etiquette

- If you're invited to someone's home, it's polite to bring a small gift, such as sweets or flowers. Don't bring alcohol unless you're sure the host drinks it. Always present the gift with both hands as a sign of respect.

Table Manners

- If you're invited to a Turkish home, it's polite to wait for the host to start eating before you do. Also, it's customary to finish everything on your plate as a sign of appreciation for the food.

Travel Tips And Hacks

Packing Tips

Comfortable Walking Shoes

- Istanbul is a city best explored on foot, especially in areas like Sultanahmet, the Grand Bazaar, and the waterfront. The city's streets can be uneven and sometimes cobblestone, so packing comfortable shoes for walking is a must. Choose shoes that are supportive and durable to avoid blisters or foot pain during long days of sightseeing.

Modest Clothing for Religious Sites

- If you plan to visit mosques, including the famous Blue Mosque and Hagia Sophia, it's important to dress modestly. For women, this usually means covering the shoulders, arms, and legs. Carry a lightweight scarf or shawl to cover your head when entering mosques. Men should also avoid wearing shorts inside these religious sites.

Layered Clothing

- The weather in Istanbul can be unpredictable, so packing clothes that can easily be layered is a smart choice. In the summer, it can be hot during the day and cooler in the evenings, while in the winter, temperatures can drop quickly. A light jacket or sweater can help you adjust to temperature changes.

Sun Protection

- Istanbul gets plenty of sunshine, so don't forget to pack sunscreen, sunglasses, and a hat to protect yourself from the sun. A good sunscreen is essential if you're out sightseeing during the hot summer months.

Power Adapters and Chargers

- Istanbul uses the standard European plug (Type C and Type F) with a voltage of 220V. If you're traveling from a country with different plug types or voltages, make sure to bring a power adapter and possibly a voltage converter.

Travel Essentials

- Pack a good daypack or small bag to carry your essentials like water, a map, snacks, and a camera during daily outings. Also, a reusable water bottle is a good idea, as it helps you stay hydrated throughout the day.

Navigating The City

Public Transportation

- Istanbul has an efficient public transportation system, including buses, trams, ferries, and the metro. The best way to pay for public transport is by using the Istanbulkart, a rechargeable travel card that works on all modes of transport. You can purchase and top up the Istanbulkart at kiosks or vending machines located in stations.

Ferries and Bosphorus Cruises

- One of the highlights of visiting Istanbul is taking a ferry ride across the Bosphorus. There are public ferries that operate regularly between the European and Asian sides of the city, and it's a pleasant way to take in the stunning skyline of Istanbul. You can also opt for a Bosphorus cruise to see more of the city from the water.

Taxis and Ride-Sharing

- While taxis are available in Istanbul, they may not always be the most reliable or affordable option. Traffic in Istanbul can be heavy, and drivers may not always use the meter. If you take a taxi, make sure the driver uses the meter before starting the trip.

Walking

- Many of Istanbul's top tourist spots are close to each other, so walking is often the easiest and most enjoyable way to get around. Be prepared for some uphill walks in areas like Sultanahmet, where the famous mosques and Topkapi Palace are located.

Use Maps and Navigation Apps

- Istanbul is a maze of streets and neighborhoods. While some areas are easy to navigate, others, like the Grand Bazaar, can be confusing. It's helpful to use a navigation app like Google Maps or Maps.me to get accurate directions.

Staying Safe

Be Cautious in Crowded Places

- The major tourist sites, like the Grand Bazaar or Taksim Square, can get very crowded, especially during peak seasons. Be mindful of your belongings and keep an eye on your bag to avoid pickpocketing. Consider using a money belt or a small, secure bag that you can keep close to your body.

Use Only Licensed Taxis

- If you need to take a taxi, make sure it's a licensed one with a visible taxi sign and a meter. You can also ask your hotel or a reputable business to call a taxi for you to ensure it's a reliable one.

Watch Out for Scams

- There are a few common tourist scams in Istanbul, such as overly friendly individuals who try to lead you to shops or offer guided tours for high prices. Politely decline if you're not interested and be cautious about handing over money to strangers.

Emergency Numbers

- In case of an emergency, the general emergency number in Turkey is 112, which will connect you to police, fire, or ambulance services.

Health and Safety

- Tap water in Istanbul is generally considered safe to drink, but if you're unsure, it's better to stick to bottled water. If you have any medical conditions or allergies, it's a good idea to carry your prescriptions and necessary medications. Istanbul has many pharmacies and hospitals that can provide assistance if needed.

Respect Cultural Differences

- Although Istanbul is a modern city, it is still rooted in conservative cultural values, especially in neighborhoods outside the tourist centers. Be respectful of local customs and dress codes, especially when visiting religious sites.

Useful Apps And Tools

Istanbulkart

- The Istanbulkart app allows you to check the balance of your transport card, find transportation routes, and make it easy to top up your card from your phone.

Google Maps

- Google Maps is an essential app for navigating the city, helping you find directions, walking routes, and public transportation options.

Moovit

- Moovit is another great app for public transportation in Istanbul. It offers real-time updates on bus, tram, and ferry schedules and helps you plan your route efficiently.

GetYourGuide

- If you're looking to book tours or activities, GetYourGuide is a popular app that lists guided tours, boat trips, and entry tickets to major attractions like the Hagia Sophia and Topkapi Palace.

Uber

- If you prefer to use ride-sharing services, Uber operates in Istanbul and is a convenient way to get around the city.

XE Currency

- XE Currency is a useful app for checking exchange rates if you're dealing with foreign currency. It can help you track current rates to avoid getting charged more than necessary when exchanging money or shopping.

HappyCow

- For those with dietary restrictions, HappyCow is an app that helps you find vegan, vegetarian, and vegetarian-friendly restaurants around Istanbul.

TripAdvisor

- TripAdvisor is helpful for finding reviews on hotels, restaurants, and attractions. It's great for getting the inside scoop on places to visit or dine in Istanbul.

Offline Maps (Maps.me)

- If you're worried about using mobile data or don't have an internet connection while in Istanbul, the Maps.me app allows you to download offline maps of the city and navigate without needing an internet connection.

Appendix

Emergency Contacts

Emergency Number for Police, Fire, and Ambulance:

- **112**

   This number connects you to emergency services, including police, fire, and medical assistance.

Tourist Police:

- **0212 527 4500**

   This number is useful if you're a tourist and need help with lost items, scams, or any issues related to tourism.

Ambulance Services:

- **112**

   For medical emergencies, you can call 112 for an ambulance.

Lost and Found (Istanbul Metropolitan Municipality):

- **153**

   Call this number if you lose personal belongings or need assistance in locating lost items in public areas.

Maps And Navigational Tools

- **Google Maps**

  This app is widely used for both driving and walking directions. It provides accurate, real-time directions and can help you find public transport routes as well.

- **Moovit**

  A great app for public transportation. It helps you with real-time updates on buses, trams, metros, and ferries in Istanbul.

- **Maps.me**

  If you don't want to use data, Maps.me offers offline maps, allowing you to navigate the city without an internet connection.

- **Istanbulkart App**

  This app works with the Istanbulkart travel card, allowing you to find routes, check your balance, and top up your card.

Tourism Centers And Locations

Istanbul Tourist Information Center (Sultanahmet)

- Address: Sultanahmet Square, 34122 Fatih, Istanbul
- Services: Free city maps, brochures, event information, and helpful staff for general travel queries.

Taksim Square Tourist Information Center

- Address: Taksim Square, 34437 Beyoğlu, Istanbul
- Services: Maps, tourist brochures, information about nearby attractions, and tours.

Addresses And Locations Of Popular Accommodation

Four Seasons Hotel Istanbul at Sultanahmet

- Address: Tevkifhane Sokak No. 1, Sultanahmet, 34110, Istanbul
- A luxurious hotel located near major landmarks like the Hagia Sophia and Blue Mosque.

The Marmara Taksim Hotel

- Address: Taksim Square, Beyoğlu, 34437, Istanbul
- A stylish hotel right in the heart of Istanbul's shopping and entertainment district.

Sirkeci Mansion

- Address: Emin Ali Paşa, Taya Hatun Sk. No:5, 34112, Istanbul
- A boutique hotel near the Topkapi Palace and the Sultanahmet area.

Addresses And Locations Of Popular Restaurants And Cafes

Nusr-Et Steakhouse

- Address: Sandal Bedesteni, Zorlu Center, Beşiktaş, 34340, Istanbul
- Known for its high-quality meats and unique serving style, this restaurant is famous worldwide.

Café Ara

- Address: Akarsu Caddesi No: 1, 34433 Cihangir, Istanbul
- A cozy café with great coffee and delicious snacks, located in the artistic Cihangir neighborhood.

Sultanahmet Köftecisi

- Address: Divan Yolu Caddesi No: 12, Sultanahmet, 34110, Istanbul
- A historic eatery famous for its Turkish meatballs (köfte) and traditional Turkish dishes.

Addresses And Locations Of Popular Bars And Clubs

For those interested in Istanbul's nightlife, here are a few popular bars and clubs:

360 Istanbul

- Address: İstiklal Caddesi No. 163, Beyoğlu, 34420, Istanbul
- A rooftop bar and nightclub offering stunning views of the city, cocktails, and live DJ performances.

Babylon

- Address: Şehit Muhtar Mahallesi, İstiklal Cd. No: 7, 34435, Istanbul
- A famous music venue known for live performances and an eclectic crowd.

Klein Club

- Address: Süleyman Nazif Sokak No. 3, Beşiktaş, 34330, Istanbul
- A trendy nightclub with a great music selection and vibrant atmosphere.

Addresses And Locations Of Top Attractions

Hagia Sophia (Ayasofya)

- Address: Sultanahmet, 34122, Istanbul
- One of the most famous historical landmarks in Istanbul, originally built as a church, then a mosque, and now a museum.

Topkapi Palace

- Address: Sultanahmet, 34122, Istanbul
- The former royal residence of Ottoman sultans, known for its impressive courtyards and collections.

The Blue Mosque (Sultanahmet Mosque)

- Address: Sultanahmet, 34122, Istanbul
- Famous for its beautiful blue tiles and architectural grandeur.

Grand Bazaar

- Address: Beyazıt, 34126, Istanbul
- One of the world's largest and oldest covered markets, filled with shops selling everything from jewelry to spices.

Addresses And Locations Of Book Shops

For book lovers, Istanbul has several great bookshops to explore:

Galata Bookstore

- Address: Galata Tower, Bereketzade, 34421, Istanbul
- A well-known bookstore offering both Turkish and foreign-language books.

D&R

- Address: İstiklal Caddesi No: 175, Beyoğlu, 34437, Istanbul
- A large chain of bookstores that offers a wide variety of books, music, and films.

Addresses And Locations Of Top Clinics, Hospitals, And Pharmacies

Here are some important healthcare facilities in Istanbul:

American Hospital

- Address: Güzelbahçe Sokak No. 20, Nişantaşı, 34365, Istanbul
- One of Istanbul's top hospitals, offering high-quality medical care.

Florence Nightingale Hospital

- Address: Abide-i Hürriyet Caddesi, 34381, Istanbul
- A well-known medical institution in Istanbul with a wide range of healthcare services.

Pharmacy (Eczane) near Taksim Square

- **Address**: Taksim Square, Beyoğlu, 34437, Istanbul
- A reliable pharmacy located near the central Taksim Square, offering over-the-counter medicines, healthcare products, and pharmacy services.

Addresses And Locations Of UNESCO World Heritage Sites

Historic Areas of Istanbul

- **Address**: Sultanahmet, 34122, Istanbul
- This UNESCO World Heritage Site includes significant landmarks such as the Hagia Sophia, the Topkapi Palace, the Blue Mosque, and the Hippodrome, all located in the Sultanahmet area. These sites represent the rich history of the Byzantine and Ottoman Empires and their architectural accomplishments.

The Zeyrek Mosque and the Surrounding Complex (Zeyrek Camii)

- **Address**: Zeyrek Mahallesi, 34400, Istanbul
- This former Byzantine church, which was later converted into a mosque, is a prime example of Byzantine architecture and is part of the historical fabric of Istanbul.

The Archaeological Site of Troy (Troy)

- **Address**: Hisarlık, Çanakkale, 17100, Turkey
- Although slightly outside Istanbul, this ancient city is historically tied to the stories of Homer's *Iliad* and remains one of the most important archaeological sites in the country. It is a UNESCO World Heritage Site that reveals the layers of history from various civilizations.

Printed in Dunstable, United Kingdom